In Search for the Soul of International Business

In Search for the Soul of International Business

Michael R. Czinkota

Georgetown University
University of Kent

BEP BUSINESS EXPERT PRESS

In Search for the Soul of International Business

First published in 2019 by
Business Expert Press, LLC
222 East 46th Street, New York, NY 10017
www.businessexpertpress.com

ISBN-13: 978-1-94944-311-0 (paperback)
ISBN-13: 978-1-94944-312-7 (e-book)

Business Expert Press International Business Collection

Collection ISSN: 1948-2752 (print)
Collection ISSN: 1948-2760 (electronic)

Cover and interior design by Exeter Premedia Services Private Ltd., Chennai, India

First edition: 2019

10 9 8 7 6 5 4 3 2 1

Printed in the United States of America.

To Ilona, who helps my soul survive and
Margaret, my Hoya Saxa!

Abstract

There is a New World Order for trade and globalization. Political and international issues metamorphose in the business ecosystem, in ways that penetrate everyday life and influence expectations beyond imagination. Inundated with constant information, new concepts, and endless data, individuals are caught in the whirlwind of a fast-paced world, often without the ability to stop and think, particularly when it comes to issues of the soul.

I consider the soul the center of our activities and inspirations. If one says about an individual that "his soul has left him," one connotes death. This also will apply to societies and corporations. Losing one's soul is a reflection of the end game. Are we willing to permit the gradual march toward solitude with all the accompanying sharp cutting edges? Will the balloon go up? The reader can judge. I hope to supply the content here.

With a foreword by Ambassador László Szabó, a preface by the Rev. Horkan, and the humorous yet pensive illustrations by award-winning cartoonist David Clark, this book epitomizes the ability to gain a comprehensive understanding of the most pressing international business and trade issues that the world faces today. Thought provoking, witty, and innovative, *In Search for the Soul of International Business* offers ground-breaking insights and perspectives to inspire real-life understanding and soulful applications in the business and marketing realm.

Keywords

faith; freedom; Georgetown University; global trade; globalization; good soul; heart; international business; marketing across borders; new world; policy; quality; terrorism

Contents

Foreword

Now This Is Interesting

Dr. László Szabó

Dr. Szabó is the ambassador extraordinary and plenipotentiary of Hungary to the United States.

Books are meant to have a mission and an impact. Just like with those who are called, some books are, while many are not. The difference lies in the interest level. Here is how my interest progressed. When I first read the name of the author, I was reminded of an eponymous suburb within Budapest. So I drew the connection to Hungary—a link that is almost reflectively appealing to a Hungarian ambassador in the United States. The title of this book adds a crucial dimension of humanity to business—it is a search for essentials in which many of us engage. Particularly appealing was the soul, which, as a former medical and business professional and especially as a diplomat, one does not connect instinctively. I decided to venture a closer look as I discovered that the author is not only a business professor at Georgetown University, one of the leading Jesuit Universities in the world, but also has an appointment at the University of Kent in Canterbury, the seat of the Church of England. After decades of being a key author of International Marketing and Business, the Professor had now seen fit to newly write about a new and crucial dimension of humanity. Society often describes business as soulless, technology and artificial intelligence might even further distance business from the soul. In all, this book raised my interest to such an extent that I agreed to write a prologue about it for you, the reader. As an ambassador, one of my goals is to strengthen business ties between Hungary and the United States. I would like to see businesses flourish that have multidimensional levels of depth and a natural concern for a good soul, so that these connections can be meaningful, long lasting, and honorable.

In conversation about the book, Professor Czinkota indicates that his primary focus is the soul, particularly the good one. He defines his conceptual innovation to be the link of faith with the issue of "curative marketing." Religious connectivity with commerce has had an important role for ages. There is, for example, the cleansing of the money changers from synagogue by Jesus and the dimension of the honorable merchant, already developed by the German Trading Group Hanse in the 13th century.

Working on international business for 40 years, Czinkota's work provides a rationale why merchants should be reliable, trustworthy, and bridge-building partners, which he has subsumed under the heading of "curative marketing." He highlights in his work that passage of time will lead to forgiveness of misdeeds under existing statutes of limitations, but does not eliminate responsibility. Even after 25 years, three generations, or even centuries, there remains an obligation for active consideration of restitution. An example is the efforts by Georgetown University to seek forgiveness and make good for its selling of slaves more than 200 years ago—Even though doing so had a major effect on the continuing viability of the institution. The descendants of the victims, as far as identified, have now been provided with enhanced access to higher education and help with their social progress. The search continues!

The concurrent step-up is the integration of the soul with international business. In times of controversial industrial measurements, highly unpleasant passenger removal by airlines, and threats of terrorism, many deplore the apparent lack of a soul in business life. Today we are facing a greater capability and willingness to bear down on conditions which warrant doing so. We retain our appreciation of old content, but also gain new perspectives and witness a new context. We can let freedom lead business, and use tariffs to improve trade conditions. Donald Rumsfeld, former U.S. Congressman, youngest and second oldest person to serve as Secretary of Defense, Counselor to the President, and White House Chief of Staff stated: "there are known 'knowns,' which are the things we know that we know. Then there are the known 'unknowns,' which are the things that we now know that we don't know. There are also the unknown 'unknowns,' which are things of which we do not know that we don't know them." As befits the soul, Czinkota's book manages to address, if not tackle, all of these conditions.

Thought provoking, witty, and innovative, *In Search for the Soul of International Business* offers groundbreaking insights and perspectives to inspire real-life understanding and soulful yet trailblazing applications in business and marketing. Consistent with the focus of this book on quick learning I hope to have, within a few pages of thought, raised your wonderment about the triple helix of business, faith, and society sufficiently so that you are now appropriately interested in reading this book of tantalizing brevity. Happy reading!

Preface

Where Is the Soul?

Rev. Edward Horkan

"Where is the Life we have lost in living? Where is the wisdom we have lost in knowledge? Where is the knowledge we have lost in information?" So asked the great poet T.S. Elliott in 1934. These questions are more applicable now than ever, in a time when so many people and so much of society are exclusively engaged in so-called practical pursuits of advancing in the world, knowing the latest fads and trends, and pursuing the gods of wealth and technology. We need to take a step back and ask, as Blessed Pope Paul VI and Pope Emeritus Benedict XVI did in their encyclical letters *Populorum Progressio* (1967) and *Caritas in Veritate* (2009), what makes for real development and progress? Is it simply having more wealth and technology? Or should we not adhere to what Pope Paul VI called a "full-bodied humanism" that "will enable our contemporaries to enjoy the higher values of love and friendship, of prayer and contemplation, and thus find themselves." Should business and politics not have a higher calling than merely gaining more wealth or satisfying more desires? Can we not, as Pope Emeritus Benedict advised, make such things as love, friendship, beauty, and the call to immortality, the overriding "principle not only of micro-relationships (with friends, with family members or within small groups) but also of macrorelationships (social, economic, and political ones)." Can business and politics not have a soul?

In this book, Professor Michael Czinkota gives advice about how international businesses can have a soul that promotes such human development. In so doing, he avoids the superficial and limited categories of so-called liberal and conservative, left-wing and right-wing thought. Thus, for example, he recognizes the important place of free markets and international trade, but also puts such aspects of society in their rightful place, namely, of developing not merely profits but also such things as trust, virtue, and friendship. With 35 articles, mostly from the last two years, he presents a perspective of how conducting business according to higher values is good, not only for human development, but also for business itself. Thus, for example, he points out in chapter 1 that business that seek a holistic development of society will find themselves at a competitive advantage because that is what customers are increasingly seeking as well. And he describes in chapters 5–9 how building trust, friendship, and the development of the whole person are essential in keeping customers and promoting cooperation among employees. Likewise, he describes in chapters 3, 4, 14, and 30, among others, how respect and understanding for other people's cultures is critical in successful international business and how international trade and investment can make each nation's culture more unique and free.

Because people in the modern world are often busy and find it difficult to read large tomes, Professor Czinkota expresses his views in one- or two-page articles that can be read when one has a few spare minutes. (He advises reading them before getting to bed so that one wakes up more informed.) The articles are mostly organized to proceed from general principles to specific issues. Thus, section I covers the overall ideas of how businesses and societies should develop such principles as responsibly for society, trust, mutual respects, and even gift giving (see chapter 6). Section II summarizes the call to develop the soul of each person and business; and applies these insights to specific business international business issues such as Brexit, antidumping duties, international tax systems, visas, and even different approaches to art (chapter 15). Section III develops at more length a specific topic, namely, dealing with terrorism, to describe how a serious challenge to international business can encourage a broad perspective on human development. Thus, for example, he describes several times how flexibility in one's business design and knowing many areas and people prevents terrorists from closing down a business by shutting off its only supply or outlet for a good or service. And he describes in chapter 22 how a concern for security against terrorism and a concern for the poor should be allied interests. In section IV, Professor Czinkota then takes on some current issues, especially those of the Trump Administration, such as the proposal to increase tariffs, trade with Cuba, and medical tourism, arguing that the central consideration should not only be the impact on productivity, but also on such things as cooperation, innovation and, as he says in chapters 33 and 35, "truthfulness, simplicity, expanded participation, and personal responsibility."

On that point, Professor Czinkota concludes the book with an analogy to Jesuit training. As Jesuits are sent into the world as "soldiers of God," we should train our bodies, minds, and souls to be more than "bean counters." Rather we should be soldiers for such causes as truth, simplicity, participation, and responsibility, which are also the basis for a truly democratic society, a theme of chapters 2 and 3. In so focusing on greater goals, even business itself will be more efficient, more satisfying, and better able to last into an uncertain future. As Jesus says elsewhere, "Seek first the kingdom of God and its righteousness, and all else will be given to you besides." Matt 6:33.

Author: Rev. Edward Horkan is a priest of the Diocese of Arlington and pastor of Our Lady of the Valley parish. He graduated from the University of Virginia in 1990 with a B.A. in Economics and a Minor in English Literature. He then earned a J.D. from the University of Virginia Law School and practiced tax and employment benefit law with Groom and Nordberg, a Washington, D.C., law firm, for four years before entering seminary. Fr. Horkan attended Mount St. Mary in Emmitsburg, MD for one year and the North American College in Rome for four years. In Rome, Fr. Horkan earned a S.T.B. and an M.A. in Spiritual Theology from the University of St. Thomas, also called the Angelicum.

Acknowledgments

My Thoughts Go To...

Researchers Dina El-Saharty, Lisa Burgoa and Yang Feng. My gratitude to my Georgetown colleagues, Professor Ronkainen, Professor Cooke, and Professor Skuba, and all my collaborators. I will always be grateful to the late Professor Bernard LaLonde for setting me on the right track. I thank Gary Knight of Willamette and Valbona Zeneli of the Marshall Center in Garmisch. Their insights and debates keep international business alive. Thanks for the economic kindness of the editors and publications who gave me permission to reprint my articles. Heartfelt thanks to David Clark, the award-winning artist, who has provided the visual stimuli for this book. Most of all, I am grateful to my wife Ilona Czinkota who is a major arbiter for the quality of my writings. Early or late in the day, she is willing to provide suggestions. My daughter Margaret comments as well with much enthusiasm and interest. Both mother and daughter are great sounding boards and come up with excellent questions and solutions. Thanks to all of you, Hoya Saxa!

Introduction

Why You Should Read This Book...

As a professor, I provide a long-term perspective of issues, campaigns, and phenomena. Going beyond the flavor of the month and conveying an overview of inner emotional content is the key purpose of this book. We can learn from the performance of body and soul, not only by understanding what was done before us but also by appreciating the changes that do and will occur. The format of less than three pages of text and a picture per chapter allows the reader to avoid a major study. Policymakers and firms have taught me that most people do not read academic books or even high-quality journal articles. Working one's way through the literature is typically considered too laborious, insufficiently stimulating, and too time-consuming. However, decision-makers do read short articles and commentaries. Therefore, this book presents an important opportunity to communicate, to bring issues to the fore, and to precipitate refined understanding.

This book offers my cutting-edge thinking about the good soul and its link to core issues of international business and trade. The thoughts presented here offer an array of themes, ranging from terrorism to business strategies. I intend to provide the opportunity to step on pillars, which provide a perspective far beyond one's accustomed circles. The view conveys the thoughts and emotions of diverse human groups and souls. I reflect how international business reaches every corner of our world today and affects the souls of individuals, firms, and societies. This book makes complexity more accessible by presenting key topics, their analysis, and controversies. The format suggests bedtime reading so that when you wake up, you will be the smartest person in the room. If you fall asleep during the read, you'll still get a bonus for partial absorption. Knowledge will be the only side effect.

People expect good medicine to taste bad. Many also anticipate informative articles to be dull, wrong-headed, and boring. There is no such requirement and I do something about it. The articles here are fun to read and make you understand important future issues in context. Through the parsimonious use of the word and the frequent offer of art, I hope to generate interest and enhance understanding, with the proverbial less than a thousand words.

In our global community, in many ways, we often miss out on commonality. Independent thought should reflect the presence and absence of a good. This reminds of the Bavarian beer and Brez'n experience where visitors fearlessly occupy any free seat around the table and accept the existence of joint intentions. The need for and acceptance of the soul gives us a common path and provides a joint perspective underpinned by a broadly supported objective.

History permeates our perspective, even if we don't know about it. We complain about the contemporaneous phenomenon of pirates in Somalia, though such profession was riding high in Sicily during Roman times. We bemoan the disruptions from terrorism but neglect that the Crusaders already wrote home about their fear of terror. We debate new approaches of artificial intelligence in teaching and communication but don't recall the effects of Gutenberg's printing press of 1440, wireless telegraphy, or the introduction of radio had on business and society. We deplore the differentiation of groups based on religion but conveniently forget the impact of Torquemada, the Inquisition, or the reactions to Luther's theses on the church doors of Wittenberg.

Consider how different things will be in a mere 50 years from today. The ballpoint pen only came to the U.S. market in 1945, the computer game Pong entered in 1972, and e-mail on personal computers only advanced in the late 1980s. Will we look as retrograde to our descendants as our ancestors appear to us today (if we bother to look)? Will they have a new view of the soul? Does that matter?

Nowadays, one discusses and often reevaluates the meaning and adjustment of key traditional business pillars such as risk, competition, profit, and ownership. Many of today's business executives gradually discover that their activities are but one component of society. The soul and its emotional subcomponents such as politics, security, and religion are only some of the other dimensions that society at large, historically, holds in higher esteem than economics and business. Those who act and argue based on business principle alone may increasingly find themselves ignored.

Think of the human condition as a sphere where one slice is business affecting and being affected by other dimensions, be they medicine, education, or thermodynamics. The overarching umbrella is the desire for shelter provided by the soul, which affects judgment, and offers simplicity. It allows the understanding of truth and enables good decision-making in light of changing realities. For example, negotiators who lose tend to blame their loss on the corruption and nepotism of winners. Yet, culturally, the closeness to family and desire to help one's own environment can be seen as obligatory rather than a deviation. Consider rules that, even though they are axioms, need a sounding board to affirm their veracity. Even aspirin may eventuate shortcomings!

Some insist that government should intervene to help create jobs, while others argue that government has already overstepped its boundaries. This book touches on the natural ebb and flows in life. It talks about the soul and innovation, which often inspire new business policies. Recessions are not seen as a signal of decline on the world stage but rather as an opportunity to move forward in new directions with new determination, and in pursuit of different rules. For example, if one demands that government provides the greatest protection possible, then we have to be willing to give up a certain amount of privacy. The acknowledgment of the soul helps to delineate limitations. Just as a river connects the two sides, which it touches, it also separates its two banks. The soul also performs a major catalytic role. Its lack can lead to a tragic loss. The emergence of public mores and scrutiny of injustice in an international context encourages companies and governments to reduce corruption and abandon unsavory practices. They listen to their soul.

This book outlines some of the far-reaching consequences of international conflict and reconciliation. Trade can be a tool to deal with crises. From refugee flows, spy wars, to the macro conflict of global terrorism, all affect and should be affected by the soul. The book elaborates on how the international good soul plays an essential role in strengthening freedom, quality of life, and progress. Do read this book, it will be fun, easy, and worthwhile. As a bonus, come visit my blog MichaelCzinkota.com, and I will share my latest thinking!

PART I

On Touching the Good Soul

CHAPTER 1

The Soul and the Curative Marketing Concept

Three score and 17 years ago, Joseph Schumpeter regaled us with the concept of creative disruption. He presented successful innovation as only a temporary market shift, which, though threatening the profits of old firms, was itself facing the pressure of new competitors commercializing their own inventions. Such continuing cyclicality was taken on in greater detail by various subfields in business and society and delivered high explanatory value. Consider the link between transportation capabilities and market reach. See the time–service linkages developed by Hollander's "wheel of retailing." He postulates that firms tend to start at the bottom of the wheel and move up in terms of services and pricing until more efficient competitors transition them out from the wheel.

Today, disruption has become broader in scope with more new entrants, and with their disruptions coming not just from the same industry or even from similar business models. A representation of disruption reflects a continuous flow of newly entering players emanating from different countries and regions. To countermand aggression, it is no longer sufficient to force besieged firms to simply lower their prices. Nowadays, there can be entirely different products, which deliver better value to consumers. Unicorn companies, like Twitter and Netflix, are startups valued at more than US$1 billion within a very short time. Unicorns have succeeded and caused many casualties with their winner-takes-all market approach. When Netflix emerged in 1997, with its lower price and convenience, it quickly permanently overtook Blockbuster, the video rental firm. With its 10,000 retail stores, the firm was forced to declare bankruptcy in 2010.

But with the world becoming more dynamic and divided than ever before, security and religion appear to be held in higher esteem by society than economics and business. Corporations are increasingly expected to play a stronger role as a collaborator with government and society in finding solutions to often-unforeseen future challenges. Winner-takes-all competition begins to give way to a strategy based on global collaboration. Money no longer is the only or ultimate outcome of business efforts. Firms who neglect holistic perspectives and argue based on business principles alone may increasingly find themselves on the losing end. Self-sufficient, societally supportive, and leading is how many business executives like to see themselves. Yet, their activities are only one slice of a floating sphere formed by a score of other components integral to society.

This is one key reason for the emergence of the concept of curative marketing, which accepts responsibility for particularly international problems that marketing has caused. It then uses marketing's capabilities to set things right even for the long term and works to increase the well-being of the individual and society on a global level. Curative marketing's two key perspectives consist of looking back at what marketing has wrought and looking forward to set things right for future relations and actions. Curative marketing provides the concept and context for the assessment of participation.

CHAPTER 2

Freedom and Globalization: Simultaneously Possible

(With Valbona Zeneli)

Globalization, trade, and investment deserve our "thank you" for their achievements. Yes, currently, in Europe and the United States, popular discontent is forcefully expressed. An introvert trend has emerged, fed by nationalism, populism, xenophobia, and antiglobalization rhetoric.

Globalization is not new; it has existed for centuries. What is different today is the speed of globalizing the world, made possible by new technologies, transportation networks, media, and international marketing.

Many claim that never before in history has there been so much evidence about strong opposition to globalization. However, any comparison with the past is highly inaccurate. Only few records of resistance to globalization have been preserved for us today.

One main feature of globalization in our age is the conveyance of freedom, which in turn becomes the foundation of good life. There are three dimensions to this freedom. For one, the opportunity to collaborate with others, streamline processes and procedures, and increase the variety of products and services cause great freedom of choice. There is the freedom conveyed by sovereignty, where nations and their governments maintain and exercise preferences for their citizens. Individual countries will always seek to have sovereign freedom. Then there is the freedom of principles and options.

Such freedom of choice is primarily expressed by the recourse to deeply rooted principles that provide the boundaries of the playing field. If there is no limitation and no alternative, then there is no freedom. A true alternative requires a decision and the exercise of virtue. If there are no principles to which one can seek recourse, there is no freedom.

In reciprocal causality, freedom both causes and facilitates international marketing, while international marketing is a key support of the cause of freedom. The focus and aim of international marketing is on crossing borders, with the goal of providing more choice for consumers and letting them be the ones to maximize their satisfaction. International marketing does so in all corners of the globe, the glamorous ones as well as in the small and remote ones where its efforts are not seen by others.

When the long-standing rivalry between socialism and market economy came to an end, market forces directly improved human rights and the extent of freedom. Exchanges through markets have clearly demonstrated greater efficiency and effectiveness in their ability to satisfy the needs of people. Now they must demonstrate their ability to persist through continuity and balance.

In spite of complaints about slowness of change, biases in wealth distribution, and economic disparities and inequalities, a majority of the participants in market-oriented conditions are now better off than they were before. World poverty has been reduced significantly. Only 25 years ago, almost two billion people, 43 percent of the world population lived in extreme poverty with less than $1 a day. Today, the poor have been reduced to 700 million people, or 9.6 percent of the world population that live with less than $1.9 a day. Research shows that globalizing developing countries grew 3.5 times faster than non-globalizing ones, over the last decades. Average incomes per capita have more than doubled in the last 25 years, from $4,192 in 1990 to $10,433 in 2015, and have increased 13 times from the 1970s, when they had an average income of $802.

One of the main discontents of globalization are low incomes in formerly successful regions, a high level of inequality within and between countries, and between the world's economic classes. People at large will not tolerate such glaring inequality anymore.

One key dimension of freedom is to allow people outside the box. National borders are where business, government, and people usually find their limits. Freedom knows no international boundaries. It thrives on how to successfully cross national borders, on coping with local differences once the crossing is done, and on profitably reconciling any conflicts. Domestic borders limit economic expansion, while international approaches contain the freedom of much wider opportunities.

International activities encourage people all around the world. The antiglobalization narrative in Western European and the United States is caused by imbalances in both people and goods, as well as an intransigent enforcement of rules from disconnected centers. Migration and refugee pressures force people to move from rural homes into urban areas, from their developing countries into industrialized ones, and to take any measure to be relieved of wartime conditions. For both sides, little freedom is involved here. Most individuals who do the moving would much rather stay home but cannot afford to do so. The recipient countries might not want to welcome the refugees and migrants but have to do so in response to humanitarian pressures.

Globalization may have been part of what triggered some of these shifts and migrations, but it also can be instrumental in restoring the freedom to stem the tide. Globalization can provide economic opportunity and alternatives for individuals in their home countries, free from pressures to shift locations, so they can become productive economic contributors. To make globalization work, governmental, managerial, and corporate virtue, vision, and veracity are required. Trading and investment partners need to understand the current context and longer-term effect of policy and business actions taken. Joint actions based on mutual interests but also accepting divergent interests will make better outcomes not just possible but likely.

CHAPTER 3

Why International Marketing Strengthens Freedom

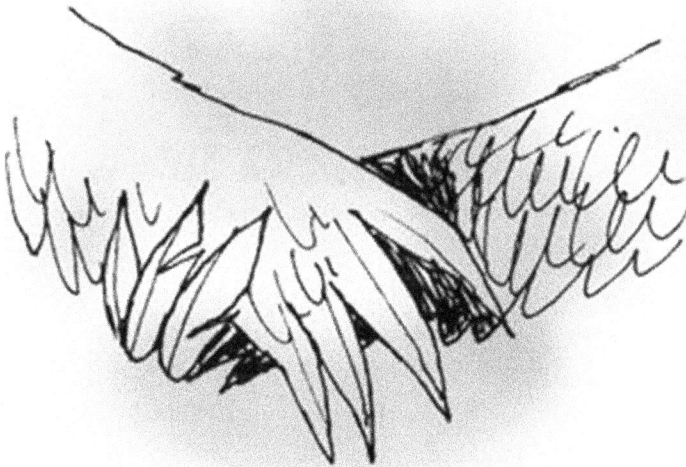

You may ask what freedom has to do with international marketing. Freedom is about options. If there is no alternative, there is no freedom. A true alternative provides the opportunity to make a decision, to exercise virtue. In the blaze of the klieg lights, it is easy to make the "right" decision. That is not an exercise in virtue, because real alternatives are effectively removed. The true selection among alternatives takes place in the darkness of night when nobody is looking.

The focus and aim of international marketing is on crossing borders. The goal is to provide more than one choice for customers, letting them pick from a selection of options in order to maximize their satisfaction. International marketing does so in all corners of the globe, the glamorous ones as well as in the small and remote ones where others do not see the efforts. By operating both in the limelight and also well outside of it, international marketing offers the freedom to exercise virtue both to the seller and the buyer—be it in decisions of supplying or purchasing, pricing or selecting.

Another key dimension of freedom is not to confine, but allow people to go outside of the box. As a concept, freedom knows no international boundaries. But national borders usually are the box where business and government find their limits. Such borders are a mere point of transition for international marketing. The discipline thrives on understanding of how to cross national borders successfully, on coping with the differences once the crossing is done, and on profitably reconciling any conflicts. International marketing contains the freedom of almost unlimited growth potential. Activities confined to domestic borders may well run into limits of expansion.

International market opportunities relax these limits quickly. Instead of restrictions, the international marketing paradigm encourages the stripping away of restraints; instead of limitations, there is the encounter of wide opportunity. Hayek thought that freedom also means not being forced to do something one does not want to do. There are economic migration pressures that force people to move from their rural homes into urban areas, from their developing countries into industrialized ones, or from wartime conditions to peaceful environment. Industrialized nations, in turn, speak about immigration pressure. For both sides, little if any freedom is involved here. Most individuals who do the moving would much rather stay home but cannot afford to do so due to major exigencies. The recipient countries might not want to welcome the migrants but do so in response to political and humanitarian pressures.

International marketing may have been part of what triggered some of these migrations, but it also can be instrumental in stemming the tide. It can provide the economic opportunity for the individuals at home so that they need not migrate. Thus, it lets individuals become productive contributors to the global economy free from pressures to shift locations. When the long-standing rivalry between socialism and market orientation was resolved, market forces and the recognition of demand and supply directly affected human rights and the extent of freedom. With all humility and gratefulness, we can conclude: Markets were right! In country after country, market forces have demonstrated typically greater efficiency and effectiveness in their ability to satisfy the needs of people. International marketing has been instrumental in stimulating these newly emerging market forces. In spite of complaints about the slowness of change, biases in wealth distribution, and the inequities inherent in societal upheavals, a large majority of participants in market-oriented conditions are now better off than they were before. Without the transition provided by international marketing, these changes would not have come about that swiftly and efficiently.

One keeps hearing about the large segment of the world population that is poor and therefore supposedly excluded from any international marketing efforts; the World Bank calls them the three-billion $3-a-day poor. By contrast, international marketers should see them as an attractive $9 billion-a-day opportunity for valuable transactions. What is more is that international marketing provides the opportunity to acquire resources without the deployment of force. Why fight if you can trade? Countries that have been historic enemies such as France, England, and Germany are now all united in collaboration through international marketing. The field is, therefore, at the very least contributing to freedom from war while providing additional choices and freedom for consumption.

CHAPTER 4

Culture Awareness Matters

Culture defines the behavior patterns that are distinguishing characteristics of members of a society. It gives the individual an anchoring point, an identity, and codes of conduct. Culture has 164 definitions, but all of them accept that culture is learned, shared, and transmitted across generations. Cultural awareness in business has been recognized over several centuries. When the East India Company came and initiated the spice trade in India in the 17th century, its members embraced Indian cultural values in order to integrate with society and promote business. To be effective marketers across cultures and borders, companies must recognize that cultural differences exist and then adapt their approach to marketing accordingly.

As many parts of the world embrace globalization, there is also a growing fear that cross-border products threaten one's cultural heritage. Without the understanding of cultural norms, marketers face the risk of invading local traditions and customs. Some of the elements that marketers need to be sensitive to are religion, language, and values. One must adapt to different cultures and respect traditions before making important business decisions in the international market. The process of acculturation—adjusting and adapting to a specific culture other than one's own—is one of the keys to success in international operations.

To compete with the local companies who are advantageously armed with the knowledge of dealing with local customers, international marketers need to win the trust of locals by respecting their culture when selling products. Pizza Hut continues to be a big success in the South Asian market. Their top-seller pizza flavors in India and Pakistan are *Veggie Supreme* and *Chicken Tikka*. This shows that the brand has not only addressed the cultural preferences but also the religious sentiments by adjusting to local markets. Today, Pizza Hut is recognized and trusted more than even local pizza brands because of its earnest efforts to appeal directly to its market.

Culture is one of the most challenging elements of international marketplace. However, once successfully accepted, the journey can become extremely rewarding. Factual knowledge can be learned but the interpretation of culture comes only through experience. Cultural awareness continues to be the cornerstone of marketing in expanding beyond local borders. Pizza Hut is just one example of a company that has successfully navigated its operations abroad through understanding its competition, audience, and culture. This proves that cultural awareness and acknowledgment in conducting business internationally can shape the destiny of companies.

CHAPTER 5

From Body to Soul: United Airlines to Volkswagen Engines

"The soul leaves the body" is a common euphemism for death, but what about "when the soul leaves business?" This is increasingly the case, as business managers care more about the bottom line than about decency and curative behavior. As I explore in my article in *Qualitative Marketing Research*, business must change: the soul must come back home.

Wrestling for the soul of business is nothing new. Each year we are reminded about just how far some companies are falling short. In 2015 Volkswagen cheated emissions regulators. United Airlines recently bloodied a passenger while dragging him from a plane the company had overbooked. Most stunning to me is that not a single United employee—pilot, ground crew, or flight attendant—interceded to say, "This is not right."

The traditional pillars of business—risk, competition, profit, and ownership—are insufficient for the modern age. Companies focus too much on hedging risks, ousting their competitors, maximizing profits, and expanding assets, and forget the cardinal rule of human decency: reverence for others. Business without soul takes on a sinister character, which charges exorbitant rates for on-flight pillows or hotel minibar snacks. To me, business is meant to create value, for itself and the customer, not leach off others.

There was a time when managers cared about all these things. Years ago, a Japanese firm I was familiar with was dissatisfied with five product failures in a 12,000-item shipment. The company demanded that the supplier conduct an investigation into its production process to prevent future problems. Their supplier was dismissive, offering instead 20 free units as compensation. The company stood firm, demanding a commitment to flawless excellence or their contract would be cancelled. The investigation took place, and the product continues to be superior. Perhaps *Profiles in Courage*, the 1957 book by John F Kennedy, needs to be reread today.

Furthermore, the old pillars need refurbishing, placing a seat on top to give the customer his rightful priority. The new pillars should be Truthfulness, Simplicity, Expanded Participation, and Personal Responsibility. When problems arise, managers often obfuscate, develop complicated excuses, or disengage by claiming "I didn't know, I just work here." Managers must take responsibility for the effects of their businesses, and initiate curative action for past damage and to prevent future harm. Not all conditions can be presented in an employee handbook. My acid test question is: "Does your mother know and approve of what you do?"

How to instill these new pillars in business? One solution is to promote mindfulness in corporate life. It is easy to lose sight of what is important, spending each day laboring in an office far from the impacts of work. Practicing mindfulness and meditation can help overcome this.

Another is to specifically focus on how to bring the soul back into business curriculum. For this, we can look to the tenets of the Jesuits, whose vigorous promotion of honor and service deserves our praise and emulation.

If businesses are to thrive in this era, they must rediscover their soul. We need companies like the old GM—a car company of car people. Passion and commitment to excellence must drive business, not bean-counting. This is the soul of business, and just as the body dies without its soul, so does business.

CHAPTER 6

St. Valentine's Day—More than Dates and Roses

For centuries St. Valentine has been the patron of love and lovers, providing individuals with the nudge to move a relationship forward. International shipments of red roses have enriched the economies of Colombia, Ecuador, and Kenya by hundreds of millions of dollars. This is the time to revisit Valentine's Day as to its meaning and make plans to restructure its impact.

Valentine's Day has already undergone significant expansion. Its celebration has grown from a small parish to half of the globe. It has become, in some of the wealthier countries, an important gift-giving occasion. Gifts have become differentiated by gender. Men consistently give more than women; perhaps because they wish for a foundation, while many women see decoration. The typical gifts are jewelry, roses, or dinner. As reported by the National Retail Federation of America, more than $810 million worth of Valentine's Day gifts are given to pets.

The timing of Valentine's Day has expanded as well. In Korea and Japan, romantic gifts are given on March 14, one month later than in the United States. The product pallet has become more diverse: for example in Denmark, instead of roses, one exchanges pressed white flowers. In the Philippines, on February 14, small events are increasingly supplanted by large ceremonies and mass weddings. Italians, instead of smelling the roses, listen to the reading of poetry and eat chocolate hazelnut kisses also known as *baci*. In South Africa the name of a beloved one is written on one's shirtsleeves.

Some governments consider the Valentine's Day as unreligious and ban its celebration. By contrast, increasingly, on Valentine's Day one does not just recognize the one you love, but also family and friends. The Pope in Rome has been known to carry flowers with him on that special day.

In sum, Valentine's Day has taken on a wider mission, diversified its outreach, and introduced more flexibility in terms of timing, product, message, and interaction with more people. Most importantly, it has propagated quite successfully the message of interaction, proximity, hugs, and love.

The next step should encourage this expansion and integrate it more with our lives as business people, policymakers, or consumers. Here are some suggestions how Valentine's Day as a widening construct can serve to incorporate present-day realities and future-day outlook. To nudge things along, recommendations are included for appropriate commemorative gifts.

For President Trump: A cake with many candles but little sugar for providing many occasions of hope, change, and new perspectives.

For Kim Jong-un of North Korea: a candle signifying the love of your people and in appreciation for not blowing up nuclear devices.

For the U.S. Congress: A "like" card for constituents to send to their own representative; to be accompanied by a "you can do better" card for the rest of the institution.

For the global trade community: A "tough love" card, which allocates specific responsibilities for rules and tasks to be changed, accompanied by jovial if not hearty messages indicating that "we understand."

For Prime Minister May: some nontear tissues—to dry the eyes—we won't break away.

For people both domestic and foreign who were struck by natural disasters or poverty: a red envelope with a check inside.

For tax payers: no plastic but a paper bag; their reductions are more than just crumbs.

For corporations: a colorful map showing new investment opportunities with large benefits.

To the Twitter company: some tightly packed characters showing concern.

For media: some loosely sourced but highly emotional news stories showing respect.

To the world at large: the form of messages and hugs represent how different cultures take different approaches to love; to get there, a relationship has to come first; joint efforts will help.

To my personal small world: humongous love to wife Ilona and daughter Margaret; your gift; anything you want.

TO ALL: Happy St. Valentine's Day!

CHAPTER 7

For Marketing, Christmas Is a Growing Global Phenomenon

Historically, the religious tradition in the United States, based on Christianity and Judaism, has emphasized hard work, thrift, and a simple lifestyle. These religious values have certainly evolved over time; many of our modern marketing activities would not exist if these older values had persisted. Thrift, for instance, presumes that a person will save hard-earned wages and use these savings for purchases later on.

Today, Americans take full advantage of the ample credit facilities that are available to them. The credit card is such a vital part of the American lifestyle that saving before buying seems archaic. Most Americans feel no guilt in driving a big SUV or generously heating a large house.

Christmas is one Christian tradition that remains an important event for many consumer goods industries in all Christian countries. Retailers have their largest sales around that time. However, Christmas is a good illustration of the substantial differences that still exist among even predominantly Christian societies.

A large U.S.-based retailer of consumer electronics discovered these differences the hard way when it opened its first retail outlet in the Netherlands. The company planned the opening to coincide with the start of the Christmas selling season and bought advertising space accordingly for late November and December, as retailers do in the United States. The results proved less than satisfactory. Major gift-giving in Holland takes place, not around December 25, Christmas Day, but on St. Nicholas Day, December 6. Therefore, the opening of the company's retail operation was late and missed the major buying season.

From a marketing point of view, Christmas has increasingly become a global phenomenon. For many young Chinese, Christmas is not regarded as a religious holiday but simply represents "fun." Fashionable bars charge up to $25 for entrance on Christmas Eve, and hotel restaurants charge $180 for a Christmas Eve function. The week around Christmas is the top grossing week for movie theaters in China, as young Chinese head out to theaters together instead of watching pirated DVDs at home. Santa Claus is increasing in popularity in the predominantly Sunni Muslim country of Turkey. In Istanbul shopping centers, children stand in line to sit on Santa's lap and ask for gifts. Stores sell Santa suits and statues.

With billions of people celebrating Christmas and exchanging wishes of peace, perhaps we will see at least some of the inspired and faithful take personal steps that reduce the barbarities humanity commits against itself in the many ongoing wars. Also, a time of remembrance of the difficult travels of Joseph and Mary, with Jesus soon to be born, might help us soften our stance against refugees and migrants in the world. Remember, we all—but for the mercy of God—could be the ones looking for succor and support.

CHAPTER 8

The Impact of Trust Bridges on Business

(With Courtlyn Cook)

Trust bridges are increasingly emphasized in business relations and partnerships. They not only help to fight corruption, but also establish a sense of community that binds people together. Corruption continues to be a hot issue in business and is more prevalent than most people acknowledge.

The baseline standard of corruption, defined by the nonprofit Transparency International, is an "abuse of entrusted power for private gain." The group sees corruption as the pursuit of selfish, individual gains and the desire to get ahead. Of course, corruption is an individual, as well as a corporate choice. Transparency International's latest study reports that 25 percent of people used a bribe in the past year, which means that corruption infiltrates a significant portion of business transactions, which is crucial to take into consideration.

Corruption interrupts corporate culture because it destroys previously established trust that has been earned on a long-term basis. Trust is a valuable corporate asset since it typically translates into fulfilled expectations, which allow for better forecasts, less uncertainty in the future, and more realism.

Trust bridges, developed by shared expectations and experiences, allow people to get to know each other quicker, and help establish fair business practices on global terms. Thus, trust is one of the best ways to combat corruption. Connections that bring people together and lead to greater trust can be built upon a shared alma mater, military service, same work experience, sports fans for the same team, and even practicing the same religion. People are more likely to bond over these personal preferences and organizations because they already share a similar interest; therefore they expect to share similar values.

If two companies operate in similar environments and share values, they are more likely to connect and establish warm and trusting relationships. This ultimately establishes credibility and allows business to select patterns based on trust rather than strictly on proximity or financial measures. Trust is developed through interaction, although there are other spillover effects that come into play. An example would be two organizations that are led by former sports champions might be more likely to trust each other, particularly when it comes to sports. This may also connote but does not necessarily require trust in financial matters.

It is important to note that trust is an extension of confidence, so high expectations often accompany trust. One such trust-enhancing activity is especially present in the German model for developing trust, which due to its reliance on standardized training and internships, focuses on keeping processes flowing due to confidence in and reliance on other's work. In contrast, less training in the United States often leads to a lack of trust and little confidence in work. Therefore trust bridges may not be as visible in the American corporate world.

Political connections often have a greater impact on communities that experience very little corruption. This means that people are not relying on bribes or other forms of under-the-table compensation to make business and personal decisions. Also, this may partially explain research on municipalities, which found that established trust bridges led to government growth and increased profitability of firms.

Relationships that are rooted in trust discourage people from engaging in dishonest behavior. One can therefore argue that corruption inhibits the foundation of relationships. When discovered, corruption can ruin a reputation. Once trust bridges are destroyed, they are difficult to rebuild.

In today's global economy that is ruled by rapid, as well as constant, communication and connection through technology, global trust standards can converge where people hold each other to the same standards. This makes international business easier because it reduces the necessity of local standards, which often results in greater costs for companies since they have to meet different standards in every country of operation.

If a global standard were in place, every country would more likely partake in international business interactions, and therefore would have a better chance of establishing trust bridges. Additionally, companies and managers making crucial decisions based on current trust bridges need to exercise less oversight. All this translates into more effective and efficient use of resources. Thus, trust bridges not only reduce the likelihood of corruption, but also lead to more efficient and profitable business transactions.

PART II

On the New World

CHAPTER 9

The Soul: Where Modern Society Fails

Business is part of society. It paves way for sustainable development in the future but its impact and "market share" are changing. The crucial pillars of business leading to stability have traditionally been measured like the four legs of a stool. A business is composed of risk, competition, profit, and ownership. Their interactions were seen as complex but necessary for the successful growth of business and even societal ventures. Today, these pillars need to be redefined because they no longer sufficiently sustain the corporation and the present world.

But shifts come about, and the discipline of marketing is the most affected. A key tenet of marketing is reverence for the customer. However, firms often choose a predatory approach, which at Georgetown some have labeled inappropriate, unjust, and counterproductive "vampire marketing." Typically, this takes place when the key consumption decision has already been made, but circumstances allow for additional offers. High minibar charges in a hotel or pillows for rent on an airplane may serve as examples.

More importantly, the failures of the companies' soul not only cause the loss of profit and reputation but also reduce the trust of consumers. In 2008, a milk scandal in China with the tainted infant formula of Sanlu Group involved 300,000 victims and four deaths of babies, which eventually led to the bankruptcy of Sanlu one year later. In a diesel emission scandal in Germany, Volkswagen (VW) affected 11 million of consumers with a test defeat device installed to cheat government tests of performance. Within one year, the cost and penalties, which resulted from public scrutiny, surpassed since we go for an international market, the United States is important. Perhaps use USD $16 billion. Severe declines in reputations and credence, leading to judicial steps against Volkswagen's former CEO, Winterkorn and imprisonment for the head of the subsidiary Audi, took the cost well beyond $22 billion. In the United States, Wells Fargo fired 5,300 employees for illegally intervening with customer accounts to obtain personal bonuses.

An insufficient guiding soul of business often brings deleterious financial impact to business. The way companies are guided and shift directions seems to be fundamentally slow. A firm without a soul seems to be inhibited from taking new actions, which should have been directed by cognizant managers responsive to deep problems.

CHAPTER 10

New World, New Policy

There are often heated discussions on trade policy shifts. To make reasonable arguments, we must consider that the fundamental composition of trade has been changing. For example, from the 1960s to 1990s, the trade role of primary commodities has declined precipitously, while in parallel, the importance of manufactured goods has increased. This has meant that those countries and workers who had specialized in commodities such as rubber or mining typically fell behind those who had embarked on strengthening their manufacturing sector. With sharply declining world market prices for commodities and rising prices for manufactured goods, commodity producers were increasingly unable to keep pace. Some commodity-dependent countries realized temporary windfalls as prices of oil, wheat, and corn rose dramatically, only to watch them evaporate as prices dropped in 2009.

More recently, there has been a shift in manufacturing to nations, which are newly emerging in the world market as both customers and suppliers. In the mid-1800s, manufacturing accounted for about 17 percent of employment in the United States. This proportion grew to almost 30 percent by the 1960s, only to decline at a rising rate. In mid-2009, U.S. manufacturing employment fell to 9 percent, with the loss of some 2 million manufacturing jobs in the recession. The decline continues until 2014. Despite this loss in employment, the U.S. manufacturing industry is in the process of significant transformation as productivity gains and skill upgrading have created a leaner and more skilled manufacturing workforce. We need to consider that due to innovation a smaller-sized workforce can manufacture more and better products. For example, U.S. value-added manufacturing output has been increasing even though there have not been major increases in employment or number of facilities. The U.S. share of global manufacturing output has remained stable at about 25 percent over the past two decades.

Manufacturing changes during that time were not confined to the United States. In the past 30 years, German manufacturing employment has dropped by 13 percentage points, while in Japan the decrease was 6.5 percentage points. Such shifts in employment reflect a transfer of manufacturing away from traditional manufacturers toward the emerging economies. During the times of large decline in the United States, Germany, and Japan, the proportion of manufacturing in gross domestic product (GDP) has more than doubled in Malaysia, Thailand, and Indonesia, helping their economies and global participation grow. Considering the large scale of benefits that so have been transferred, it is sensible to ask whether such economic transfers need to continue to be subsidized by the United States and other key industrialized nations. In an era of freedom and global opportunity most countries should be able to use their own resources to support their growth, and understand the possible disadvantages emanating from trade or investment overhangs.

CHAPTER 11

Brexit and the United States

International trade and investment issues grow more complex and require major reconsideration by governments, firms, and individuals. No one is exempt from the new policy directions of the U.S. government and the impending British exit (Brexit) from the European Union (EU). They are accompanied by extensive security concerns and the need to manage vast immigration flows. Many of the accompanying political battles are not only driven by national options, but reflect the "because we can" principle. While U.S. policy changes are still under construction, Britain delivers the EU separation documents consonant with Article 50 of the Treaty of Lisbon by the end of March 2019, which then marks the bureaucratic starting point of Brexit.

Americans have typically been isolated from many events and threats by two mighty oceans. New World and New Policy affects the United States and Europe simultaneously. There are major changes in business relations within the EU, and important effects on culture on both sides of the Atlantic. Some say that rather than walking the walk of diversity, we are ominously close to a road of divisiveness. What then is necessary to avoid a dramatic deterioration of global civility, security, and economy? Understanding and preparation will not remove the thorn of separation but may help reduce the pain of adjustment.

The British separation encourages other nations to seek acceptance of their special desires as well. But when there is a reallocation of payments and supports, who will be the beast of burden and at what price? Also, what is the role of innovation and timing? As the United States discovers, being the first with good ideas and their implementation does not always pay off.

The self-inflicted British exit can weaken the economic relationship between the United States, Britain, and the European Union. A UK departure shifts the entire European unification from an outlook of optimism and growth to a fear of long-term division. Britain's significance as a business cluster is declining. Less demand for currency will keep the value of the pound and of non-Euro currencies low, but also gives their governments more ability to adjust and manage their currency and trade accounts. Relative salaries, housing prices, innovation, and new ventures will become less robust. The plans of many people to establish their life in Britain will change. Inward tourism may rise but outward travel will suffer.

Fascinating on a psychological level is the fact that most people, on either side of the Atlantic, continue in a very protective phase of denial when looking at possible effects, both short and long term. Such a limited focus restrains the willingness to prepare, since "it just won't happen here to me." Time will tell about the wisdom of the reduced response rationale. In the interim, the signs "We are European" may help shore up a countermovement to Brexit.

Trade and investment issues already thought settled will require revisitation and new access accords. New negotiations will be harder since all participants remember how things used to be but are not bound by that.

To many the cost of renegotiations seems wasteful. But not adjusting to new conditions will risk instability to which Iceland can attest. The volume of new trade diplomacy and its collateral implications will produce new forms of negotiation, particularly close links to forecasting, and new formats of standardization, robotization, and global subcontracting.

American outward foreign direct investment (FDI) will change. Every day almost one million people go to work in America for British companies. More than one million people go to work in Great Britain for American companies. Under new conditions, these numbers might shrink.

Both the United States and Britain require new relationships that are less organized by tradition but more individualistic and spontaneous. Social media can play a big role here. Also, highly emphasized traditional business fundamentals such as competition, risk, profit, and ownership will have to be modified in favor of truthfulness, simplicity, expanded participation, and personal responsibility.

Friends and adversaries do not require winners and losers. With all the physical, technical, and information resources now easily available, we must search for the spiritual soul of business, and make it catch up with the physical body. We all must contribute to finding new paths to help others by sharing their burden. They in turn must be willing to share ours.

It used to be said that a common language only separates the United States and England. The near-term future may see more separation of the two by new negotiations. There is the opportunity to improve relations with new negotiators who are not only rear-view-mirror-oriented, risk-averse or restrictive. Using past configurations as milestones can help simplify future trade policy, but without mandatory orientation. Bilateral discussions between the United States and the UK must focus on the building of strength. Global openness with reasonable partners, accompanied by transparency, and in support of balanced consumption are key objectives for progress toward a better human condition.

CHAPTER 12

Dumping Penalties: Give to Caesar What You Owe to Caesar

US president Trump has issued a new executive order focusing on international cheaters, who do not pay their debts due to dumping penalties. The order targets the problem of unpaid special customs duties known as "countervailing duties" (CVD), levied on products from companies found guilty by an "antidumping" investigation.

First to the jargon: "Dumping" refers to a type of predatory trade practice. In its simplest form, it amounts to a company selling a product in a foreign market for less than it costs to make it. In theory, the goal of "dumping" is to drive down the price, and in doing so, muscle out smaller, weaker competition in order to later establish a monopoly status on that market. Under the rules of the World Trade Organization, dumping is a prohibited practice, and countries are permitted to levy special taxes on goods found to be unfairly dumped in their market in order to rebalance the price level. These tariffs are called "countervailing duties," abbreviated as CVD.

The United States currently has filed 379 Anti-dumping (AD/CVD) cases. The largest number deal with various steel products, as well as agricultural and manufactured goods. Of the culprits, China is in the lead with 142 pending cases. At issue in the executive order is a problem brought to light by a 2016 report from the Government Accountability Office (GAO). The GAO report noted that only about 30 percent of the duties assessed and owed are ultimately paid, resulting in approximately $2.8 billion in unpaid levies. The report notes the majority of these are owed by the largest importers, and some 90 percent of the unpaid duties are owed by Chinese companies.

The facts seem to support President Trump's views on trade. These companies are "cheaters" who take advantage of the US market, but don't comply with its rules. They deserve to be punished, since by selling to a country that offers them vast business protections, and then by flaunting its laws, they add insult to injury.

We also need to keep this order in context. It requires Customs and Border Patrol to enact stricter and higher bonding requirements on imports. Companies owing duties must "post higher bail" at the border to import their goods. There will be results. Yet, it is also important to bear in mind the scale of the evasion, which is only about one half of one percent of the overall trade deficit. Nonetheless, as behooves good business practices, every bit counts.

The symbolism of this order may be more important than the substance. After all, if a domestic firm were to engage in "dumping" or sell their goods below cost, we would call it a "sale" benefiting the customer. The timing of the order is also noteworthy—only a week ahead of an official visit by Chinese president Xi Jinping. This order may have been posturing ahead of their meeting, as President Trump aimed to extract concessions from the Chinese. Every bit counts!

CHAPTER 13

What Do I Owe Ya?

President Trump announced a new executive order aimed at pushing forward his trade agenda. Targeting the US trade deficit, the order directs the Commerce Department and the US Trade Representative to lead an interagency investigation and produce a "comprehensive report" on the causes of the US trade deficit. They are to do so by looking at specific industries and trade policies by foreign countries that contribute to the continuing gap between US exports and imports.

According to the US Census data on trade, the United States ran about a $500 billion net trade deficit in goods and services with the rest of the world in 2016. The United States runs a larger deficit when looking only at goods (such as manufactures, agriculture, etc.), at $750 billion, while the county runs a surplus of about $250 billion in services (such as business services, finance, information technology, etc.). Broken down by country, the largest goods deficits are with China (over $54 billion in the first two months of 2017) and Mexico, as well as Saudi Arabia (petroleum imports) and the European Union. In services, it is noteworthy that the United States runs sizable surpluses with all of these countries.

As the Trump administration looks to improve the U.S. trade position, the underlying presumption of this executive order is that these trade deficits may emanate from unfair practices on the part of U.S. trading partners. Unfair impediments could range from prohibited subsidies, inappropriate barriers to US exports, or manipulation of exchange rates. In order to create jobs, bring in more fairness to exchanges, and update mutual relationships, the president's executive order plans to provide an empirical basis for an anticipated newly equilibrated trade policy. After all, it has been 70 years since the global trade institutions still in charge today were designed and implemented.

It will be important to clearly understand what deficit numbers mean. Take the example of Saudi Arabia. Despite recent increases in domestic oil production thanks to fracking, the United States remains a net importer of oil. We weaken the doctrine formulated by Henry Kissinger in 1970 to keep U.S. oil reserves in the ground if possible and import from others willing to deplete their stock. That way, Dr. Kissinger declared, we will hold crucial reserves for emergencies. In an era of new technologies, such a shift in doctrine makes sense, but it does also affect national security concerns if rapid shifts are required.

Published trade numbers do not show underlying supply chains and cross-border value-added activities. Ever since the 1994 creation of North American Free Trade Agreement (NAFTA), many U.S. companies, such as the auto industry, have developed cross-border supply chains. Parts and components are produced in the United States and shipped to Mexico, where they are assembled and shipped back to the United States as a finished car. Under current accounting, Mexico runs a surplus as their export is measured as the whole value of the car. This "deficit" hides the real value of the trade—cheaper cars for consumers, more domestic jobs for producing components, and higher wages for our neighbor to the South, which in turn reduces immigration problems.

As Commerce and Presidential office of the United States Trade Representative (USTR) get ready to dig into the trade numbers, they may not like all they'll find—"deficits" tell only part of the story, and many American jobs count on the global supply chains and resource imports. Doing a comprehensive research on trade and its limited reporting is valuable input for future new policy formulation. This is also the time for our allies and trading partners to come forward with their trade data insights to help make the picture clear, complete, and transparent.

CHAPTER 14

How Psychic Distance Impacts Trade

The U.S. trade deficit is large. In 2016, it was more than $500 billion and it will remain high in the coming years. Policymakers should be deeply concerned about our country's long-term economic health.

Two major approaches can improve the international trade position of the United States. The first is to reduce imports, and the second is to increase exports. U.S. customers appear, at least in the short run, unlikely to reduce their consumption from abroad. So one needs to find ways to increase exports.

Companies are said to develop the direction of their export thrust based on their "psychic distance" to other countries. This concept, as defined by researchers at the Uppsala School, consists of two dimensions: cultural and geographic factors. People and companies are considered to be more "culturally distant" when there are differences in customs, language, and economic development. People and companies are regarded as being "geographically distant" when they are further apart only by sheer mileage.

The theory of psychic distance has significant implications when applied to the export process. Exporting begins among people and companies that are less culturally and geographically distant. For example, Canadian companies present the opportunity for U.S. companies to work with a country that has both cultural similarities and geographic proximity. U.S. companies ultimately can transfer this experience by expanding into new markets that may be more psychically distant to the United States.

One could attempt to reduce the psychic distance between countries to enhance trade relations. For example, a U.S. business executive could visit a Latin American immigrant area in the United States to become more knowledgeable of their language and customs. A deeper cultural understanding could be beneficial for this U.S. business executive when trying to handle trade negotiations with Latin American executives. If cultural dimensions become more familiar among individuals, then the psychic distance is lessened through cultural understanding and trust.

To sum up the key issues:

- Selecting a country as an export customer is the combined choice between cultural and geographic dimensions.
- To encourage exporting, it helps to start with low-hanging fruits. For U.S. firms, this is a result of the combination of both cultural and geographic proximity. Canada or the United Kingdom could be major testing regions.
- Change happens! Over time, a region may reconstitute itself, which can impact trade relations. Immigration can trigger cultural change among countries, such as language facility, psychological expectation, or new demand.

The United States must recognize the role of psychic distance and its potential impact on improving the U.S. trade balance deficit and enhancing American's economic competitiveness.

CHAPTER 15

What Art Tells Us About the Global Economy

The modern world of art offers fascinating insights into the forces currently shaping world trade and the global economic system. For decades, China has experienced breakneck economic growth and has become a world leader in both the consumption and production of art, which illustrates some intriguing changes in the global economy.

The global market for high-end, rare art pieces is a good example. In recent years, as China grew more prosperous, there has been a sharp uptick in luxury art purchases by Chinese customers. In 2016, according to insider information, Oprah Winfrey sold a 54″ × 54″ painting to a Chinese collector for $150 million. This example indicates how China has grown in its appreciation of originals. This shift perhaps presages an eventual reduction in counterfeit products for which China is still infamous. Chinese auction houses have also risen to prominence. Of the world's top 10 art auction houses, six are Chinese, and many of the largest art houses are state-owned enterprises.

In the art world, China has not only become a dramatic consumer of art, but also a prodigious producer. The southern Chinese city of Dafen, near the megacity Shenzhen, which borders Hong Kong, has become the center of knock-off art masterpieces. Beginning in the 1980s reform era, Dafen became a hub for starving artists from around the country to work and train, pumping out high-quality knock-offs of famous European and American painters ranging from Van Gogh's *Sunflowers* to portraits of Western icon John Wayne. Artists produce these works on the cheap and can offer custom alterations, such as changes to the color or size to fit the purchaser's own décor. Since the works are not signed, they do not count as fakes.

The producers of export knock-off masterpieces will face pressure to adapt, focusing more on creativity and original works. When Chinese artists copy the great masters, they hone their skills and imagination, which over time will allow them to eventually emerge as new artists in their own right.

The demand for copies of classic masterpieces at an affordable price seems likely to continue; there is no shortage of impecunious art lovers, after all. In the face of low-wage competition from China, what are Western artists to do? The answer is much the same as in manufacturing and other industries—use technology.

Art may seem an unlikely candidate for technology innovation. Advances in artificial intelligence, machine learning, and 3D printing have opened up possibilities previously unimaginable. In 2017, a tech company from the Netherlands is reported to have taught all the core elements of a classic Rembrandt painting—the style of clothes, how he draws the eye, the texture of his brush strokes—to a computer. Through deep learning software, the system was able to compose and "paint" through the use of a 3D printer a "new, original Rembrandt," a painting in his distinctive style of a person that only exists as the "imagination" of the computer.

Just as Chinese artists can produce "custom masterpieces" on the cheap, Western art programmers can push out wholly original but stylistically recognizable classics. In art as in the broader economy, the future of global trade competition will be between the low costs of labor in developing world and the productivity-enhancing technologies of the emerging nations.

China's rise from a global consumer, to the continued mass production coming from its numerous factories, and the growing significance of advanced technologies is reflected by the art world, which offers an indication of major global trends. Since changes shaping the global economy continue to accelerate, observers would be well advised to use their China-assembled iPhone to take a picture of the temporary present.

CHAPTER 16

How Tax Cuts Help U.S. Companies to Go Abroad

World trade has forged a network of global linkages, in which everyone and every country is involved. Nowadays, a drought in Brazil and its effect on coffee production and prices is felt around the world. U.S. subsidies for ethanol production from corn affects prices for other agricultural crops and livestock in the far reaches of the world. As the key player in globalization, any U.S. reform tends to change the international market. The old saying goes, if the U.S. sneezes, other nations catch cold.

After only 100 days in office, President Trump has already released a tax reform memo to the public. Although not complete and detailed, there is a clear signal coming from the release on how the government would like to encourage U.S. companies to export and invest abroad.

First, comes a cut in the top tax rate for all businesses to 15 percent, far below the current 35 percent top rate. This reduction is not imbalanced since it would also benefit the owners and shareholders of international corporations in the United States. With this tax cut, companies, especially manufacturers, can lower the price of exports, and have more money for R&D and marketing. This measure will greatly enhance the competitiveness of U.S. goods in the global market. Also, a tax reduction will significantly reduce the financial constraint on companies and allow American companies to seek investment opportunities on a global scale.

Second, there is a proposal to switch to a territorial tax system. Today, U.S. companies must pay U.S. tax on all their profits, regardless of where in the world those profits were earned. A territorial approach would require firms to only pay U.S. tax on what has been earned in the United States. For profits held overseas, the Trump administration wants to offer a one-time tax reduction opportunity, which encourages the return of capital from abroad. International profits by U.S. multinational corporations held abroad are estimated to be $2.6 trillion; without incentive, they may never be brought back to the United States. A U.S.-oriented flow will provide new capital for domestic investments to infrastructure and innovation.

This plan may seem to be an unusual proposal for a president who has championed an "America first" approach and railed against companies that move jobs and resources overseas. But when looking at it closely, we find that the territorial tax system gives U.S. companies incentives to go abroad and to obtain a growing share of the global market. For the profits held overseas, there will be a special, one-time opportunity to bring home money parked abroad. The one-time tax reduction gives companies a chance to relocate their money, rearrange the resource distribution, and adjust strategies according to the market dynamics.

President Trump is consistent with his polices from campaign to the office. This tax proposal shows a continued gain for strength of the domestic market, but also encourages the exploration of every corner in the world, to help America to be great again.

CHAPTER 17

Buy American, Hire American

U.S. president Donald Trump has issued a new executive order focusing on so-called Buy American, Hire American policies. Making the announcement at the Snap-on Tools plant in Kenosha, Wisconsin, the president's order directs various federal agencies to produce reports and recommendations on government procurement policies, with the goal of increasing domestic employment and production.

The executive order covers two broad areas of government policy: numerous "Buy American" laws and regulations, which set requirements that materials purchased by the government—say, steel for building a bridge—give preference to U.S. domestic producers; and "Hire

American," which aim to address reported abuses of H1B visas that undermine high-skilled domestic labor.

The government procurement component of the order is not surprising, given President Trump's stated plans to boost domestic production through large-scale infrastructure projects. The language of the order specifically mentions targeting materials being "dumped" in the U.S. market, a priority for the administration as I address in a previous article on anti-dumping duties. The H1B issue is also not surprising, as then-candidate Trump often criticized its abuse on the campaign trail.

Offering a little background, the H1B visa is a nonimmigrant work visa used to bring in high-skilled workers, such as doctors, scientists, or technology workers. The program is subject to various regulations, such as equal pay and documentation requirements, to avoid displacing U.S. workers. However, several high-profile cases of abuse have emerged, such as the 2015 uproar over Disney's plans to bring in low-paid foreign IT workers on H1B visas, and requiring the American staff to train them before being themselves laid off.

Part of the concern seems to be the way the visas are currently issued. H1B visas were initially intended as a means for businesses to bring over talent unavailable in the United States. The Customs and Border Patrol agency takes applications from companies up to a certain limit, and issues the visas by lottery if applications exceed the cap. Currently restricted at 85,000 visas a year, applications typically surpass the quota within weeks of the application window. As a result, the visas do not necessarily go to the most qualified candidates, but to the quickest and luckiest ones. As another unintended consequence, this system benefits large outsourcing firms that flood the applications office, crowding out the applicants for whom the program was intended.

Despite these abuses, the controversy over H1B points to a more glaring problem: the shortage of technology workers in the United States. According to a Brookings report, job postings in fields of science, technology, engineering, and mathematics (STEM) take nearly twice as long to fill as non-STEM positions. Managers from Silicon Valley, for example, argue they need the H1B to fill these types of positions, since they provide specialized skills that are not easy to find.

Concrete changes to the H1B visa will depend on the reports developed by various U.S. government agencies, but it's clear that the order aims to limit the use of the program. However, this may be missing the bigger picture. The real root of the problem is lagging STEM and computer science education, as well as insufficient practical job training programs for in-demand skills. Restrictions on foreign workers alone will not create these skills in American workers.

To see real benefits for the U.S. tech industry, the administration should aim to cultivate these skills at home to meet the growing demand for them. Otherwise, cutting off the supply of skilled labor could do more harm than good.

CHAPTER 18

Entrepreneurial Money Produces Residency Permits

A successful Chinese entrepreneur showed me a news article. It reported that wealthy Chinese could buy an American passport and become U.S. citizens. Is this really true? What are the implications of this visa program?

The U.S. Congress established the U.S. Employment Based Fifth Preference (EB-5) program in 1990, to link investment, employment, and residency. Three years later, the program language was relaxed from "to create 10 direct employment opportunities," to "directly or indirectly create 10 job opportunities." This is broad and flexible wording. It is designed for entrepreneurial and wealthy investors outside the United States, who fund a new commercial enterprise of at least $500,000 for investments. Under the program, those entrepreneurs, their spouses, and their unmarried children under 21 years old can apply for green cards permitting residency. The objective is to attract foreign investments to the United States, and to stimulate economic development and job creation.

EB-5 demand has increased rapidly. In 2012, President Obama extended the program. In May 2017, Congress extended the EB-5 Program until September 2017. There are many supporters.

In 2014, 10,000 EB-5 petitions were filed with the United States Citizenship and Immigration Services (USCIS). Overall, 5,115 applicants have been approved. Over $2.5 billion investments were attracted. An additional $6.2 billion are awaiting federal adjudication. EB-5 capital is also an attractive low-cost funding tool for project developers in the United States. It offers foreign investors a way to permanent residency that is not backlogged by other applications and does not require sponsorship by a U.S. employer.

Throughout the world today, numerous programs like the EB-5 have been established. In Australia, for example, foreign investors are granted the opportunity to immigrate, but only receive temporary residency for four years. An investment of AUD $1.5 million in an Australian company (US$1.2 million) is required. France allows foreign investors to obtain residency for 10 years by making a "long term and non-speculative investment of at least €10 million (U.S $11.8 million) in industrial or commercial assets."

There is a standard moral objection to the EB-5 program: the United States should not be in the business of selling the right to live there. This claim suffers from a slight misunderstanding. In effect, the government gives the visas away to profit-making businesses that have jumped through the program's requisite bureaucratic hoops. Then the companies can solicit investment based on the promise of permanent residency. In spite of 10,000 slots a year, 40,000 investors still wait for a green card. Obviously investor needs have not been met.

Investment immigrants are in high supply. The U.S. government should use the opportunity and open the gates to them. The United States has an immigration culture, with a spirit willing to absorb both elites and refugees of the world.

However, change must come; the program needs to be refined in terms of size of investment, number of jobs generated, industry direction, geographic location, and job recipients. I believe that the investment minimum should be $2.5 million, and the American job creation shall be at least 25. Then we can continue this program helping both investors and employees; a noble outcome!

PART III

On Terrorism and Its Impact on International Business and Trade

CHAPTER 19

Marketing Across Borders Under Conditions of Terrorism

(With Valbona Zeneli and Gary Knight)

Terrorism refers to the risk or actual encounter of violent acts designed to cause fear and intimidation. Despite posing an important threat to internationally active firms, there is a paucity of empirical research that addresses the distinctive challenges that terrorism poses to the international marketing activities of firms.

Here we first provide a theoretical background on terrorism and its effects on international marketing in emerging markets. We then relate terrorism to operational costs, marketing planning, supply-chain management, and distribution activities in multinational enterprises (MNEs).

We recognize significant costs in the international marketing budget of MNEs. Firms with substantial resources and international experience appear to have more alternatives, which allow them to cope better with the effects of terrorism than their less endowed peers.

Terrorism is a salient threat to organizational competitiveness in international marketing. It is the premeditated use or threat to use violence by individuals or subnational groups to obtain a political or social objective through the intimidation of a large audience beyond that of the immediate noncombatant victims.

For terrorists, perception matters! Terrorist attacks around the world have increased greatly in the past decades, spanning 92 countries and over 28,000 fatalities in 2015 alone. Most attacks are directed at civilians, businesses, and business-related infrastructure. The five countries most exposed to terrorist attacks in recent years are Iraq, Afghanistan, Pakistan, India, and Nigeria.

Emerging markets are particularly affected by terrorism since their businesses and citizens have less of an opportunity to protect themselves. Among the possible environmental contingencies that can affect marketing organizations—such as weak economic conditions, rising energy prices, and financial crises, terrorism is identified as potentially the most serious threat.

Since terrorists select their targets with high flexibility, intensity, and precision, international firms seek a competitive advantage through the expansion of production, distribution, and the marketing of products and services across multiple national boundaries.

Terrorism sharply reduces corporate enthusiasm to expand. Measures to counter terrorism in turn are based on restricted freedom of movement and increased government regulation, both of which impair global commerce. The border-crossing effect of terrorism creates slowdowns for international transactions reaching 2.5 percent of merchandise value, which is comparable to the average level of global tariffs.

International trade depends on the efficiency and cost-effectiveness of global transportation systems. Terrorism increases the transaction costs of international commerce and delays global supply chains and distribution channels. Terrorism's main impact reaches far beyond its immediate and direct effects. What is key is the long-term results from the indirect effects that occur in national and global economies.

These include widespread anxiety and uncertainty that affect buyer demand, shifts or interruptions in the supply of needed inputs, new government regulations and procedures enacted to deal with terrorism, and longer-term perceptions that alter patterns of global trade and investment. Terrorism can also affect managerial attitudes toward risk, shift the risk absorption capacity of firms, and reduce the likelihood of embarking on international ventures or new investments abroad.

Our Google search of the NGram viewer system analyzed the extent of terrorism-related writings, and checked for correlations with the key terms "trade," "investment," and "risk." The results indicate a rapid increase of concern about terrorism since 1998. This development serves as an indicator of the growing preoccupation (in the English-speaking literature at least) with terrorism. Concurrently, and as expected in terms of theory-based postulations, the actual risk increased while trade and investment interests declined.

We believe that terrorism will continue to be a significant factor in international marketing for decades to come. The rise of terrorism signals a new type of threat relevant to both developed and emerging economies. As governments increase security of public facilities, the likelihood of attacks against the softer targets of firms' international operations is likely to increase.

Emerging economies need to find ways to increase their security in order to retain their attractiveness for foreign sourcing and investments. Corporate preparedness for the unexpected is a vital task. Innovative managers develop appropriate resources, and undertake planning and strategies to accommodate dislocations and sudden shocks. Terrorism represents an organizational crisis whose ultimate effects may be unexpected and unknown, posing a significant threat to the survival or performance of the firm.

Terrorism presents the firm with a dilemma that requires new decision-making and behaviors that will result in organizational change. Firms that neglect to devote resources and capabilities to respond flexibly to terrorist triggered disruptions, risk sudden, sometimes even, total loss of competitive advantage.

CHAPTER 20

Time to Limit the Pay-Off for Terrorists

(With Valbona Zeneli and Gary Knight)

Terrorists want more "bang for their buck" by undertaking high-impact events, choosing high-visibility targets, and directing their violence at less well-guarded "soft targets" such as transportation systems, business, and private facilities.

Terrorism in the firm's external environment is designed to create organizational confusion and contextual volatility, which refers to discontinuous changes and requires firms to make frequent, abrupt, unexpected, and untested adjustments to their business strategies and operations. There also tends to be a perhaps misleading belief that terrorism responsive decisions must always be made swiftly.

Terrorists deliberately target noncombatants and insufficiently protected physical facilities. The globalization of commerce, travel, and information flows have enhanced the ease with which terrorism can be carried out and increased the visibility and availability of potential terrorist targets. Port facilities, industrial clusters, shopping centers, and financial districts are among numerous assets susceptible to terrorism via low-tech approaches. The threat is especially salient to firms with business facilities and infrastructure in multiple and diverse locations abroad, each one of which may need tailor-made protective measures. When evil doers make multiple-tap asynchronous attacks, losses can exceed worst-case scenario planning. Institutions and firms of industrialized nations are most vulnerable when they operate in emerging countries. Multinational Enterprise (MNE) supply chains are vulnerable to potential long-term harm, particularly with firms whose first and second tier suppliers stretch around the world, in and out of risky environments. Any physical movement of goods introduces risk, disruptions, and delays, but in developing nations more so.

Perceptions of threats from terrorism reduce the likelihood that firms will expend assets abroad, particularly in emerging economies that might become terrorism-prone areas in future. Companies spend billions annually to manage terrorism-induced risk and comply with terrorism-related government procedures and regulations.

Uncertainty is an attribute of marketing environments, particularly in international markets. Marketing activity is vulnerable to terrorism through disrupted international logistics, supply chain and distribution activities, insufficient information flows, and growing global demand for industrial and consumer goods. The complexity formed by linkages among terrorists, producers, buyers, and public actors reflects how with only three to four alternatives for each option, terrorism represents hard to control and large numbers of scenarios. Furthermore, terrorism can trigger imposition of new regulations and procedures, which can hamper corporate activities. Security can reduce but not eliminate terrorism or fully insulate the firm from attacks. Government regulations aimed at preventing terrorism generate delays and increase the cost of business transactions, affecting corporate competitiveness.

The marketing organization comprises a bundle of strategic resources. Abundant material and effective alternative capabilities are traditionally associated with superior performance in international marketing ventures. The payoff from strategic resource stock piles is only realized when management activates situation-specific organizational responses and behaviors, aligning them with clear and present changes in the corporate environment, not before.

The resource-based view (RBV) helps explain how firms develop and leverage organizational capabilities. Management structures, bundles, and leveraged resources determine the efficiency and effectiveness of company operations and organizational performance and robustness. The allocation of available marketing resources and the creation of new types of marketing tools are fundamental to the creation and maintenance of sustainable competitive advantages. Our research has found that many firms remain ill prepared to cope with terrorism, especially those operating in emerging markets. Firms often still respond passively or only reactively to the onslaught of terrorism. By contrast, we encourage firms to create proactive and innovative solutions for the management of terrorism threat. This is what corporate innovation should be all about.

Such innovation must permeate organizational culture and be supported by new knowledge- and technology-enabling responsiveness to new, outwardly unexpected capabilities. Indeed, strongly innovative firms have highly developed and elaborated knowledge-creation routines and learning regimes. A strong innovative culture supports the firm in developing responses tailor-made for rapid deployment with new organizational capabilities. Rather than pursue just unidimensional thinking, ready for one action, firms need to deploy ambidextrous strategies and reinvent the situation specificity of their operations. Thus, management, which possesses a strong innovative culture and substantive awareness of even marginal threats of terrorism, might emerge less scathed from attack than firms that are focused but limited in their outlook.

CHAPTER 21

Search For Corporate Effects of Terrorism

(With Valbona Zeneli and Gary Knight)

The scientific approach is largely driven by hypotheses which are analyzed as to their likelihood of being acceptable, true and robust. We present thoughts on the odds and consequences of relationships between international marketing and terrorism. We suggest arms length and reliable insights which improve our contextual understanding and decision making. Here are several hypotheses which we postulate are associated with terrorism and corporate action.

First are increases in Marketing Costs, accompanied by disruptions of supply chains. Interruptions in global supply chains tend to cause shortages or delays of critical inputs, which affect corporate strategies and performance, shrink shareholder value, and reduce the consumption of goods and services. Perhaps the entire "just in time" production processes of a firm and its supply chain may need to be reconfigured. Increased security measures heighten the complexity of motion which increases costs. Contextual volatility raises the cost of coordination, as suppliers and distributors devote more resources to environmental scanning, information processing, and negotiating with their suppliers for synchronized responses to rapid changes within all affected organizations.

For marketing planning, design, and organization we believe that an increase in the threat or occurrence of terrorism, makes management select its risk as a salient factor in the firm's international marketing planning, supply chain management and organization of global distribution channels. To develop business strategies which minimize the firm's exposure, managers tend to avoid direct investment and to require higher returns on investment. Exports can rise but with higher cost assessments for the development of new infrastructure in terrorism-prone areas. Terrorism also appears to depress buyer psychology and consumption.

International Experience plays a major role in the firm's marketing planning, and the design and organization of the firm's global distribution channels. The acquisition, interpretation and distribution of knowledge are critical for optimizing performance of global supply chains, and achieving superior resilience and market share. Reducing the firm's risk due to unfamiliarity with a market, also called the "liability of foreignness", pays off by decreasing market operational uncertainties, and shrinking surprises. It pays off to be on site, a motto which argues for multi-dexterity in international strategy. Substantial experience in numerous foreign markets is greater than the sum of its parts, and becomes a strategic asset when a firm must confront terrorism in its global operations.

Organizational Resources of the firm affect its competitive advantage. They can strengthen assets such as in-house knowledge, skilled personnel, superior strategies, and financial reserves. The ability of firms to succeed in light of international business adversity is largely a function of the resources available to explore alternatives.

Resource-restricted firms face greater challenges to create a solid business foundation by researching foreign markets and potential partners. Conversely, well-resourced firms have a greater capacity to undertake international ventures that will perform well. Therefore, we expect that firms with comparatively abundant resources will be better positioned to undertake sophisticated international marketing preparations. They can incorporate the environmentatl contingencies of terrorism into their planning, their development of supply chains, and their distribution channels, all key components of international success.

CHAPTER 22

Does Terrorism Cause Poverty? Or the Reverse?

(With Valbona Zeneli and Gary Knight)

In light of the limited empirical research of terrorism effects on the international activities by firms, we undertook a two-phased exploratory investigation. First, we conducted qualitative interviews with internationally active firms on terrorism to develop a broad understanding of what companies and managers see as the key salient issues. We also conducted discussions, generally 45 to 60 minutes in length, via telephone and at company sites, with senior managers of nine firms with extensive international operations. These interviews provided a clearer picture of managers' concerns about and response to terrorism and facilitated the creation of a survey used in the second phase of our research.

Respondents worried about interruptions of supply chains, distribution channels, and logistics due to terrorism. Concerns also focused on the trustworthiness and reliability of foreign suppliers and intermediaries exposed to terrorism. Attention also rested on corporate capabilities that allow firms to prepare for potential disruptions and delays due to terrorism, and keep resources available to protect from and counteract terrorism.

The second phase of our research was an online survey of a sample of international firms headquartered in the United States but active in many countries around the world. The survey aimed to validate earlier findings, to better understand perceptions about terrorism, and to assist with the planning and responses that managers are undertaking when confronted with terrorism.

The unit of analysis was the firm. For standardization purposes, company resources were assessed as "annual revenues per employee," where total annual revenues were divided by number of employees for each firm. We used five-point Likert scales.

In internationalizing firms, it appears that the threat or occurrence of terrorism is associated with immediate increases in international marketing costs and with disruptions in international supply chains. Management becomes likely to include terrorism as a detrimental factor in international marketing planning, and in the design of global distribution channels.

Finally, the more resources held by the firm, the more willingly terrorism and its repercussions will be recognized. The trend appears to be that particularly among informed and wealthy firms a terrorism presence creates early and significant corporate responses. Terrorism seems to be a key causal factor in fomenting poverty much more so than poverty-creating terrorism.

A significant insight!

CHAPTER 23

The International Supplier Conundrum

(With Valbona Zeneli and Gary Knight)

Terrorism exposes firms to high levels of uncertainty and risk. Growing threats produce higher costs and more disruptions for the international marketing organization. Terrorism highlights the vulnerabilities produced by global sourcing, international distribution, and reliance on independent agents abroad. Unfamiliar settings also complicate intelligence gathering and corporate governance. Yet, firms need a globalizing marketplace.

Our survey of 151 multinational manufacturing firms reveals the threat of disruptions in international supply chains. Increased costs require management to include terrorist contingencies in decision-making. Advanced planning and strategic action can provide the firm with greater resources and capabilities for managing external shocks and adverse events.

Terrorism has become an ongoing challenge and now is part of the "new normal" of international marketing. Enemy groups can access and employ asymmetrically destructive power. In addition to loss of life and property, the growing ferocity of attacks sows panic and triggers new frictions for global commerce. Thus, operational, process, and strategic innovations that shield the firm are an increasingly prudent investment.

Natural disasters and human-made ones can be mitigated by investments that help against their impact. Such spillovers need to be considered environmental scanning is a key step in the planning process.

Globalization exposes MNEs to the risk of interdependence and imposes unanticipated perils. However, superior intelligence gathering alerts the firm to vulnerable areas and assists in forecasting as to where and how terrorists will likely strike next.

In international marketing, due to their longevity and fixed locations, channels and supply chains are particularly vulnerable. Sourcing, just-in-time systems, lean production, decentralized planning, and supplier configurations, all need to be reevaluated. For firms that rely heavily on independent suppliers, management needs to emphasize increased coordination, more reliable and transparent partners, and steps to improve trust and commitment.

Enterprise resilience refers to a firm's ability to operate in risky environments and overcome discontinuities. Resilience requires flexibility, familiarity, and redundancy. To the extent that disruptions result in long-term shortages of needed materials and supplies, firms may opt to produce essential inputs themselves. Alternatively, in spite of cost, theoretical preference for single-source supplies, inputs should be sourced from a wider range of suppliers to provide for contingencies and limit exposure to risk. Even the best systems can fail under circumstances of sudden stockouts without replacement planning.

Crisis management is effective when disasters are averted or when operations are rapidly sustained or resumed. As already suggested by strategist Sun Tzu, the most effective crisis management minimizes potential risk before an event. Planning for terrorism is akin to financial investors rebalancing portfolios periodically to optimize returns and reduce risks. Management might divest risky assets and increase holdings in other, geographically more safe locations or industries. Resources liberated in this way are then re-invested to optimize the firm's risk level and absorption capacity.

Innovations give rise to new safeguards in global operations. Management needs to develop metrics that trade-off the costs and benefits of risk mitigation measures. For example, while the use of multiple suppliers is useful, it must be balanced against increased costs and the benefit of distribution circumvention. The task can be particularly complex when marketing internationally, because the foreign context introduces diverse contingencies that complicate analyses. But in a world that sometimes resembles a boiling cauldron of disruption and insecurity, such preparatory analysis is required for survival and prosperity.

So it needs to be done!

CHAPTER 24

Future Research on and Preparation for Terrorism

(With Valbona Zeneli and Gary Knight)

Concluding this series of our research findings, here are future directions for investigating terrorism and international marketing. Like the legs of a sturdy stool, there are three priority areas: the firm's value chains, its rapidity of recognizing threats, and its preparedness with responses to terrorist events.

Marketing in emerging economies searches for the most effective operations to reduce the impact of terrorism, to decrease the response time to terrorism, and to avoid market failures.

It is important to create business models that minimize interference and disruption. For example, hamburgers do not have to be distributed through burger palaces but can reach customers through outside vacuum tubes. Suppliers don't all have to come only from a few nations but can be sourced from a wide diversity of countries.

Financial efficiency must now be traded off with robustness and a cushion against disruption. The balance of benefits and costs needs to be understood: just how much does it cost to increase protection by one percent. What risks are worth taking? What are heuristic spinoff effects of traditional models, and do they need to be revisited? The new aim must be the monetization of alternative terror responsive strategies that improve performance under risky conditions. Real options theory can focus on risk uncertainty and emphasize creating and then exercising the now appropriately understood options.

Research must conceptualize and communicate the exposures of proposed investment projects. Apart from the investment benefits, one should also rate an investment for its tie-down effects expressed by the viability and cost to withdraw an investment once it has been made and the restrictive effect on strategic directions. For example, since the choice of investment locale will determine the climate in which one operates there may well be an impact on the use of car or building paint selection. Also worth examining is exogenous uncertainty in international markets that lies beyond managerial control. International marketers need flexibility for unexpected market developments. Financial options theory can help measure and quantify the effect of such management versatility.

Systems theory lets managers examine the threat and vulnerability exposures of the firm. The interdependence of networks of firms, affiliates, and agents within larger systems require examination together with how individuals relate to and interface with other actors in the socio-political sphere of interest. A systems perspective reduces the risk for management to underspecify marketing parameters. It becomes easier to understand and respond to the geopolitical environment, terrorism networks, and newly recognized sources of risk in business systems themselves, with a focus on the vulnerability of specific network nodes.

Future research should differentiate the effects of terrorism on services industries. Some aspects of services, particularly for international markets, may vary substantially from those of traditional goods. We investigated the effects of terrorism on the international operations of manufacturing firms. By comparison, firms in the services sector are often more vulnerable to terrorism. Substantially affected industries include airlines, transportation, and hospitality, as well as banks, insurance firms, and other financial actors. Most service-providing firms enter foreign markets via FDI. Services are growing in importance. They represent the fastest growing sector in international business and usually constitute the largest proportion of economic activity in advanced economies and emerging markets.

Assuring service resilience by both an industry as well as an individual person is therefore crucial and imperative for the viability of business under the threat of terrorism.

CHAPTER 25

Let the Body Catch Up with the Soul

Instead of widening the girth of the four core business pillars presented by risk, competition, profit, and property, we should consider connecting them with a sturdy seat on top, improving the stool's comfort, stability, and reach. It may be time to combine old doctrines of business-capitalism by itself with often ancient but also newly emerging insights of wisdom and philosophy. Such a connection represents a new linkage with active connectivity of the soul of business.

In the court of Solomon, during the monarchic period of the 10th century BCE, Genesis 2:7 describes that a living soul denotes a living person. Loss of soul is loss of life. Shouldn't a living soul also denote a living business? In the 8th century BCE, a royal official from Sam'al, named Kuttamuwa, ordered an inscribed stele erected upon his death.

The inscription requested that his mourners commemorate his life and his afterlife with feasts "for my soul that is in this stele."

If the soul is removed from a business, does or will the business die, or is the soul of business a separate entity, leading to a business either with or without the presence of a soul? Does the soul guide business to see and interpret itself, as already raised in the Bible? How does a soul-less business score as a whole? What is the role of timing and the soul—past, present, and future? Is there a pro-social, holistic, and humanistic effect of or by the soul? Does the role of the soul vary, both externally in the social sphere and internally in the management environment?

Christianity in the West has shed the light of Catholic moral tradition onto business ethics, with Christians endeavoring to do their duties honestly and going beyond what they must do diligently. They do not take actions simply because they can. Pope Benedict XVI wrote:

> *Christians oppose greed and exploitation out of a conviction that generosity and selfless love, as taught and lived by Jesus of Nazareth, are the way that leads to fullness of life. The belief in the transcendent destiny of every human being gives urgency to the task of promoting peace and justice for all.*

The Anglican Church wrestles with the position of companies when addressing the theme of "can companies sin?" Taoism in the East emphasizes the necessity to consciously experience oneself, listen to both one's inner voice and to the voice of the environment in a noninterfering and receptive manner. Lao Tzu tabled the concept of "Wu Wei," literally translated as "non-doing": If one leaves the people alone and lets them get on with it, social problems will resolve themselves because political interference is more often the cause of problems than their solution.

East or West, these wisdoms are inspiring the modern world and its value systems: slow down the steps of profit-making and let the soul forge new understanding. To have one or many souls isn't some business skill that is "nice to have." Rather, it provides guidance for companies to align their principles with a mission and a vision. A soul needs to be noticeable in an organization, affecting all members of the team and classifying for individuals, with almost automaticity of how business complexities will be resolved.

PART IV

On Trade and Its Future

CHAPTER 26

Great Things Can Happen, and Not Just for America

When President Trump attended the G20 meeting in Hamburg, Germany, the aspects publicly reported were mainly uncontrolled demonstrators, burning Porsche cars, and police at the end of their rope. Few benefits were attributed to the meeting. That is incorrect.

A longer term, all-embracing perspective shows important progress. Traditionally, Europeans and their media undertake little effort to learn and contemplate about U.S. plans, visions, and constraints. It's like they are measuring in meters while we measure in yards, which can lead to bias and error. The 10 percent difference might not appear large, but it sure matters in the long run.

U.S. presidents tend to be attacked on a global scale for their thinking on trade, investments, collaboration, and innovation. Many misunderstandings emanate from differences in context and background. Meetings offer opportunities to clarify, explain, and build consensus. President Trump reflects U.S. leadership when raising the need for greater circumspection in trade, investment, and defense. No longer can there be continuous special flows of funds and privileges from the United States to Europe. Times have changed and Europe has the privilege and obligation to stand on its own.

In preparation for Germany's September election, Chancellor Angela Merkel seeks to claim a leadership vision when she warns that Europe may need to assume responsibility for its own fate. Such a leitmotif invokes belated and hollow comparisons to the past due to a lack of commitment. It also bypasses progress due to a lack of implementation for the future. Aside from Trump's comments, both exploratory and forward moving, little else from the G20 meeting was long term, silo busting, or innovative.

Trump has explained before that he does his best work one-on-one with leaders, rather than in a consortium. This was demonstrated by the improved mutual relations between the United States and France. In the past, ties often have been strained. Now President Trump has developed a new rapport with President Macron with new steps to help develop a relationship in which trade and investments and joint intentions can prosper.

The French president worked his way through the crowd of international leaders to ensure his position next to Trump. The two shared a firm handshake and a hug and a smile, proving President Trump might have a way with the French after all.

There also was the ceasefire in Syria, a major win for Trump. Earlier, attempts to create peace in the bombed-out nation failed. Now we seem to have a working cease-fire agreement. The atrocities that have infected Syria for the past years have diminished. In fact, groups have rested their weapons.

This could be one of Trump's biggest achievements in the first year of his presidency. This peace treaty, if it holds, is not only a pat on the back for the United States, but will improve all global relationships.

The Trump approach aims to shape the future both of economies and countries. It sets far-ranging priorities, in which partners with good intentions rectifications and recognize their responsibilities and lead in their implementation both spiritually and financially. They also accept rectifications made necessary by shifts. Government-based on responsibility is not always fun to implement. By contrast, Europeans are much more transaction-oriented and opaque.

President Trump lives up to promises made. He maintains his support for more balanced trade relations and the requirement for all nations to pay a fair contribution for the benefits they obtain from the United States. He also aims to change formerly strained relationships to flourishing ones, not only for the benefit of international trade but for the viable maintenance and success for spheres of interest.

Change links new thinking, a new context, improved approaches, and incorporation of new parameters into newly structured partnerships. That is good and long overdue in an era of boiling liquids just below the surface. Relationships that are rigidly frozen cannot last. It is time for the emergence of new bonds and new trust bridges, which substitute for prejudice, uninformed claims, and rabble-rousing. There is also no longer room for failed treaties. Progressive positive relationships are upon us.

CHAPTER 27

Tariffs Can Be Useful

President Trump has announced tariffs against steel and aluminum imports to help domestic industries long suffering from import pressure. Pundits have bemoaned these steps as inappropriate and precursors to a trade war. But one must consider other dimensions in play, which make these announcements useful.

Think of the difficulty with which shifts in policy and diplomatic direction are implemented in Washington. Bureaucrats typically far outlast their current team of policymakers. So, it is often difficult for a well-intentioned appointee to implement change and witness its result.

Trade is only one of the economic components of government, and just one section of many parameters forming policy. New policymakers go through all the same motions as those before them, the initial touching of base, the mutual assurances of collaboration, and the plans to develop a joint vision.

But, little if anything happens. Things just chug along without new outcomes. More time brings new issues, which take priority over earlier pressing concerns. Existing trade structures may become acceptable to many leaders, which makes change even more difficult.

Change of global issues is slow in coming. To speed things up and to get results, there has to be a spotlight. Issues have to affect a number of important countries simultaneously, and lie on the surface of the policy cauldron.

For progress to occur, different issue trade-offs between countries have to be possible. There has to be some "give" in exchange of some "take." There has to be timing immediacy to move things along and to have government leaders and their bureaucracies address, analyze, understand, and endorse changes. For all this, there needs to be an anvil focus.

The tariffs open the world outlook onto a new direction: they command attention from all trading partners; they require a response instead of the typical speechwriter niceties. New thoughts on the purpose and capability of trade can lead to an active re-analysis of policy steps and agreements.

Much of today's trade understanding has been in place since the international institutions of Bretton Woods were formed in 1944. Surely, after 74 years, policymakers, firms, their long-range planners, and academics should be able to come up with some helpful innovations.

All this is likely to precipitate shifts, adjustments, and new conditions. There will be new global actions and perhaps even entirely new paths and expectations for both international and domestic business transactions, lifestyles, and relationships.

Maybe there will be more domestic vacations, shorter college times, more white asparagus, and more extended families. We just might wind up with new conditions, which make society more productive and life more pleasant.

If President Trump's announcements and communications capture the attention of world leaders, they can astutely trigger progress and new approaches. Recognizing that a crisis could happen tends to clear the mind of decision makers.

After all is said and done, the benefit of the tariff announcements lies in the attention and understanding, which trigger new processes and precipitate change. If that occurs, then the threat of tariffs is a useful means to an end. Strong admonishment with flexible rescission can make all boats rise.

CHAPTER 28

Free Trade Zones and Counterfeit Goods

The European Union Intellectual Property Office (EUIPO) and the Organization for Economic Cooperation and Development (OECD)'s recent report claims that free trade zones may be facilitating illegal activities, such as trade in counterfeit and pirated products, by providing good infrastructure with little oversight over its use.

Free trade zones (FTZs) encompass a broad range of activities, from tourism to retail sales. They typically represent duty-free customs areas, or offer benefits based on location, in a geographically limited space. Today, there are over 3,500 zones in 130 economies, collectively employing 66 million workers worldwide.

A number of benefits drive countries to embrace FTZs. In general, these areas increase a nation's foreign exchange reserves and improve the balance of payments. On a local level, new supply chains increase business for domestic producers that sell inputs by zone-based firms. Finally, these areas provide jobs that bolster employment and, at least in developing countries, can lead to higher wages over time.

Apart from FTZ's benefits to their host country at both a local and national level, there may also be economic exposure to criminal activities as a result of insufficient regulation. Research shows that the number of FTZs in an economy appears correlated with the value of exports of counterfeit and pirated products.

With less oversight, rogue actors are attracted to FTZs to engage in illegal and criminal trade. The OECD's findings indicate that one additional FTZ within an economy increases counterfeiting by 5.9 percent on average. It also appears that FTZs tend to be overly permissive by letting companies get away with poor safety and health conditions. This limited oversight is particularly troubling when one considers the potential for exploitation in areas such as human trafficking.

The OECD and EUIPO both stress the need for future action to curb the misuse of FTZs. They recommend developing clear guidelines for countries to increase transparency and promote clean and fair trade in FTZs, based on the involvement of industry members and key stakeholders of the trade supply chain.

The organizations identify three areas for future analysis. The first is the measurement the role of FTZs in the trade of illicit and counterfeit goods. The next step requires a fuller quantitative analysis of counterfeit goods. Finally, further research needs to explore why counterfeit profiles differ from similar economies.

FTZs provide a number of advantages to economies, but without further regulation and research, they may induce heightened criminal activity. Both public and private actors must devise and apply strong deterrents to the establishment of criminal networks.

CHAPTER 29

From Rome to Geneva: On the Significance of Trade

What gave Rome its preeminent power in the ancient world? No doubt its legionnaires were feared from Iberia to Galcantray. To fund military power the descendants of Romulus engaged in prolific international trade. Today, as globalization and international trade spark heated debates in capitals around the world, it is important to remember the long history of trade. From the Chinese to the Phoenicians, the Spaniards and the Dutch, the mighty British Empire and the American industrial power-house, trade has been at the center of every great power in history. Great powers can either take that which they need by force, or buy it away. To most, trade is clearly preferable.

World trade today is shaped by rules and institutions that date back to the formative period of the modern era. Rising from the ashes of the Second World War, the victorious powers considered the underlying problems that had fueled the conflict: financial instability and rampant inflation and the breakdown of the global trading system due to competitive tariff hikes. The impending victors attempted to ensure such that a tragedy never happens again. The rules they laid out still reverberate today.

At a hotel in Bretton Woods, New Hampshire, the leaders of the world met in 1944 to lay out a new order. To provide for financial and exchange rate stability, the International Monetary Fund (IMF) was formed. Hoping to avoid the Smoot–Hawley tariffs that drove the world deeper into depression, delegates conceived the General Agreement on Trade and Tariffs (GATT), a secretariat in support of meetings aiming to reduce tariffs and to promote trade. To help fund investments to rebuild and promote economic development, the World Bank was incorporated. These three institutional pillars aimed to ensure greater stability for the international economy.

So far, the world has benefited greatly from these institutions. Trade continues to promote prosperity, and trade and investment flows stretch around the world like never before. However, these rules and institutions have been far from perfect. The IMF has been a target of much criticism over its pontifications and politically unpopular conditionality in providing financial relief. Trade liberalization has been driven by the GATT successor, now called the World Trade Organization (WTO). Countries also formed regional trade blocs like the NAFTA and the EU. While trade creates winners and losers, "it all takes time" does not placate the losers of trade shifts. The ire of workers displaced by increased import competition affects attitudes and elections.

In the developed world, many take the existence of these institutions for granted. But politicians threaten withdrawal from the WTO, even if their election campaigns benefit from donations by trade supporting brands like Coca Cola, Microsoft, and McDonalds, which span the globe. Though many call "globalization" an evil 13-letter dirty word, multinational exposure typically strengthens firms. Studies show that international businesses are less vulnerable to risks, and on average pay higher wages. Globally recognized brands raise the profile and competitiveness of products.

The old saying was "all roads lead to Rome." This was more than a commentary on Italian logistics. The power of the Roman Empire derived from its extensive network of trade relations. Allies saw that it was more efficient and profitable to join them than to fight. Today, the roads all lead to Geneva, New York, and Washington D.C., the homes of the WTO, the United Nations, and the IMF/World Bank, respectively. When Rome fell to barbarians, it was not for lack of arms, but weakness from within. Trade had made Rome strong, and the decline of trade foreshadowed its fall.

Rome's decline does not mean that the United States must decline as well. The rules and institutions of the world trading regime undoubtedly require reform. The latest negotiations, the Doha Round, have lasted well over a decade with little results. Rules need to be updated to reflect economic trends like the digital economy and trade in services. Systems need reform to prevent repeating past failures like the global financial crisis.

No one, and particularly not the United States should cut itself off from the global system. Instead, there needs to be investment into workers and the development of a global mind-set among business leaders. Global prosperity requires globally competent workers. Protectionism can't achieve this. It requires better education, and encouraging the leaders of tomorrow to see the world and get international experience. All roads still carry the global trading system. Policymakers and future business leaders need to learn how to walk them.

CHAPTER 30

The Case for Cuban Engagement

After six decades of communist rule in Cuba, the island is now governed by someone outside of the Castro family for the first time since the 1959 revolution. The new leader, Miguel Diaz-Canel, was vice president and a provincial party chief.

Many believe that the political and economic status quo of the Caribbean nation is unlikely to change. However, lessons from the business world indicate that any change in an organization's key leaders ushers in a new era for a company.

Whether it's an acquisition, merger, or the appointment of a new CEO, these transformations usually carry enormous repercussions for key functions.

New priorities are typically manifested by new promotions, new players, new rules, and new aims. In turn, this results in shifting financial conditions, new private developments, and new service assortments.

When applying such transition effects onto countries, one could argue that there is an opportunity for President Trump to act decisively in formalizing and normalizing trade relations with Cuba if conciliatory and meaningful changes are made.

For example, changes could be made so that there are no longer higher hotel rates for Americans than for Europeans, as well as no more ongoing accusations or regurgitation of historic events that have long passed.

Curative international marketing, a theory developed at Georgetown University's McDonough School of Business, directly addresses past errors and focuses on long-term restitution and improvements.

Such a move would advance U.S. businesses and their strategic interests while allowing Cuban citizens to operate in the private sector independent of the communist regime.

So far in the Trump administration, the opposite tactic has been taken by restricting American travel and trade with Cuba, which is a reversal of President Barack Obama's policies.

A pro-business posture allows for increased commercial relations (beyond cigars) that would be more effective in countering the interests of the Cuban military's monopoly in business.

This policy would empower private Cuban entrepreneurs by eliminating their dependence on the Cuban state apparatus and open them up to U.S. leadership and influence in the region. Private success over public ventures would speak volumes in favor of new economic and social thinking.

As a first measure, restoring the capacity for U.S. citizens to schedule individual visits to Cuba, which was eliminated in 2017, should be considered.

The potential economic boon for Cuba's tourist industry could eventually stimulate growth in both the U.S. and Cuban economies. Also, this measure would promote democratization and bolster innovation and an entrepreneurial spirit in Cuba.

The recent promising developments in the Korean Peninsula indicate that diplomacy rather than deterrence can advance American interests in places where ideological and strategic divisions run deep. As the White House approaches a deal in East Asia, it could apply the lessons learned from the North Korean negotiations closer to home in Cuba.

President Trump's acumen for deal making can face an ultimate test in Cuba. Opening conversations and trade with the island could mark a vast improvement in the bilateral relationship. Hopefully, the American people can look forward to the use of politics that shapes a future good for all of us.

CHAPTER 31

Balance Trade by Boosting Exports Through Government Promotion

The Trump administration is attempting to lower imports in order to rebalance trade after decades of U.S. neglect toward economic relationships around the world. Rebalancing should not only be done by applying the stick of import reductions, but also by export promotion.

Exports make a firm's markets grow and change its home nation's currency value. When U.S. exports increase, the dollar typically goes up in value. Shrinking exports tend to weaken the dollar. Exports also shape public opinion of globalization and offer the opportunity for economies of scale.

Higher production volume often means a lower cost of production. Since high exports also make imports cheaper, a firm may achieve lower costs and higher profits, both at home and abroad, through exports. Exporting also allows firms to learn from their competition and improve their ability to survive in a changing environment. Domestic firms typically have an advantage in their home countries due to familiarity, connection, and local government support. Any firm that survives the burden of foreignness already has demonstrated exceptional performance.

Finally, exporting may well lead to additional international corporate strategies, such as joint ventures, franchising, or licensing. All of these strategies together contribute to the economic strength and security of a nation. The United States has many exporters. Thousands of smaller-sized U.S. firms.

They do so because of their new ability to compete. In the past, the government was able to help with the profitability of exporting, but the contemporary foreign buyer considers more than price when making a purchase decision. Consumers also expect an excellent product fit, high levels of corporate responsiveness, full integration into the global value chain, a substantial service orientation, and unrelenting corporate commitment. New and growing firms must offer direct lines of accountability and be more responsive throughout the ribs and fabric of the merchant umbrella.

Most importantly, small firm owners are more committed and integrated once they go international. Increasingly, millennial means global awareness, interest, and understanding. Yet, there are also substantial export problems for U.S. firms, particularly the small and medium-sized ones. Logistics are a big concern, particularly in reverse channel activities, like coping with consumer complaints, product adjustments, and returns. Legal procedures and government red tape are also of concern where there are substantial differences in government restraint of innovation.

The servicing of exports is also complex, where the firm needs to provide parts availability, fit into a supply chain, and offer forward-looking technical advice. Foreign market intelligence is another problem area that covers information on trade restrictions and competition overseas. These obstacles, both real and perceived, often slow down export efforts. As U.S. firms are on the path to export, they encounter rising risk accompanied by decreasing profitability.

There is typically a market gap for small firms, where you spend more but earn less, which discourages managers from starting, or continuing, to export. Government export assistance can help firms bridge this gap by getting them to a stage where profits increase and risks dwindle.

Export assistance must either reduce the risk to the firm or increase its profitability from export operations. For example, government negotiations to open markets abroad are likely to decrease the risk of the firm. Offering low-cost credit is likely to increase profitability. Our new export assistance needs clarity of purpose, including what export assistance needs to achieve and in what time frame. Export assistance needs to achieve either a reduction of risk or an increase in profits for firms. It should be concentrated in those areas where profits and risk inconsistencies cause market gaps.

Export assistance must be closely linked to domestic industries to ensure U.S. benefits for U.S. negotiations. Negotiators must pivot around government strengths, such as contract renegotiation and prowess in opening doors abroad. All this requires boldness of vision. Today is the day to ensure that things are done right and to check whether one can do more of the right things.

CHAPTER 32

Needed: A New National Export Policy

The Donald Trump administration aims to lower imports in order to rebalance, after decades of neglecting economic relationships around the world. Doing so should not only be done by applying the stick of import reductions, but also by having as its second major claw of strength and refinement the principal tool of export promotion.

Exports make a firm's markets grow and change its home nation's currency value. When U.S. exports increase, the U.S. dollar typically goes up in value. Shrinking exports tend to weaken the dollar. Exports also shape public opinion of globalization and offer the opportunity for economies of scale. Higher production volume often means a lower cost of production.

Since high exports also make imports cheaper, a firm may achieve lower costs and higher profits both at home and abroad through exports. Exporting also allows firms to learn from their competition and improve their ability to survive in a changing environment.

Firms typically have a domestic advantage in their home countries, due to familiarity, connection, and local government support, whereas firms from abroad typically have a disadvantage. Any firm that survives the burden of foreignness already has demonstrated exceptional performance.

Finally, exporting may well lead to additional international corporate strategies, such as joint ventures, franchising, or licensing. All these strategies together contribute to the economic strength and security of a nation.

The United States has many exporters. Thousands of smaller-sized U.S. firms account for a growing proportion of exports. They do so because of their new ability to compete. In the past, government perhaps was able to help with the profitability of exporting. But the contemporary buyer abroad considers not only price when making a purchase decision. Consumers also expect an excellent product fit, high levels of corporate responsiveness, full integration into the global value chain, a substantial service orientation, and unrelenting corporate commitment and responsibility.

New and growing firms must offer direct lines of accountability and be more responsive throughout the ribs and fabric of the merchant umbrella. Most importantly, small firm owners are more committed and integrated once they go international. Increasingly, millennial means global awareness, interest, and understanding.

Yet, there are also substantial export problems for U.S. firms, particularly the small- and medium-sized ones. Logistics are a big concern, particularly reverse channel activities, to cope with consumer complaints, product adjustments, and returns. Legal procedures and government red tape are also of concern, where there are substantial differences in government restraint of innovation. The servicing of exports is also complex, where the firm needs to provide parts availability, fit into a supply chain, and offer forward looking technical advice. Foreign market intelligence is another problem area, which covers information on trade restrictions and competition overseas. These obstacles, both real and perceived, often slow down export efforts.

As U.S. firms are on the path to export, they encounter rising risk accompanied by decreasing profitability. There is a market gap typically for small firms, where you spend more but earn less, which is unattractive for managers who either do not start to export or stop doing so. Export assistance by the government can help firms bridge this gap by getting them over the hump to a stage where profits increase and risk heads down.

Export assistance must either reduce the risk to the firm or increase its profitability from export operations. For example, government negotiations to open markets abroad are likely to decrease the risk of the firm. Offering low-cost credit is likely to increase profitability.

Our new export assistance needs clarity of purpose, including what export assistance needs to achieve and in what timeframe.

Export assistance needs to achieve either a reduction of risk or an increase in profits for firms. It should be concentrated in those areas where profits and risk inconsistencies cause market gaps.

Export assistance must be closely linked to domestic industries to ensure U.S. benefits for U.S. negotiations. Negotiators must pivot around government strengths, such as contract renegotiation and prowess in opening doors abroad. All this requires boldness of vision: today is the time to ensure that things are done right and to check whether one can do more of the right things.

CHAPTER 33

The United States and the United Kingdom Must Face New Work Challenges with New Policies

International trade and investment issues are becoming more complex and require major reconsideration by governments, firms, and individuals. No one is exempt from the new policy directions of the U.S. government and the impending British exit (Brexit) from the EU.

These issues are accompanied by extensive security concerns and the need to manage vast immigration flows. Many of the accompanying political battles are not only driven by national options, but reflect the "because we can" principle.

While U.S. policy changes are still under construction, Britain will deliver the EU separation documents consistent with Article 50 of the Treaty of Lisbon by the end of March 2019, which marks the bureaucratic starting point of Brexit.

Americans have typically been isolated from many events and threats by two mighty oceans.

Some say that, rather than walking the walk of diversity, we are ominously close to a road of divisiveness. What is necessary to avoid a dramatic deterioration of global civility, security, and the economy? While understanding and preparation will not remove the thorn of separation, it may help reduce the pain of adjustment.

The British separation encourages other nations to seek acceptance of their special desires as well. But when there is a reallocation of payments and support, who will be the beast of burden and at what price? Also, what is the role of innovation and timing? As the United States has discovered, being the first with good ideas and their implementation does not always pay off.

The self-inflicted British exit can weaken the economic relationship between the United States, Britain, and the EU. A UK departure shifts the entire European unification from an outlook of optimism and growth to a fear of long-term division. Britain's significance as a business cluster is declining.

Less demand for currency will not only lower the value of the pound and non-Euro currencies, but also give its governments more ability to adjust and manage currency and trade accounts. Relative salaries, housing prices, and innovation will become less robust. The plans of many people to establish their life in Britain will change. Inward tourism may rise, but outward travel will suffer.

What is fascinating, on a psychological level, is the fact that most people, on either side of the Atlantic Ocean, continue in a very protective phase of denial when looking at possible effects, both in the short and long term.

Such a limited focus restrains the willingness to prepare since "it just will not happen here to me." Time will tell about the wisdom of the reduced response rationale. In the interim, the signs "We are European" may help shore up a countermovement to Brexit.

Trade and investment issues already thought to be settled will require revisitation and new access accords. New negotiations will be harder since all participants remember how things used to be but may not be again. To many, the cost of renegotiations seems wasteful, but not adjusting to new conditions could result in instability, to which Iceland can attest.

The volume of new trade diplomacy and its collateral implications will produce new forms of negotiation, particularly close links to forecasting and new formats of standardization, robotization, and global subcontracting.

American outward FDI will change. Almost one million people in America work for British companies. More than one million people in Great Britain work for American companies. Under the new conditions, these numbers might shrink.

Both the United States and Britain require new relationships that are more individualistic and spontaneous rather than organized by tradition. Social media can play a big role here. Also, highly emphasized traditional business fundamentals, such as competition, risk and profit, and ownership will have to be modified in favor of truthfulness, simplicity, expanded participation, and personal responsibility.

With information resources now easy to obtain, we must search for the spiritual soul of business and make it catch up with the physical body. We all must contribute to find new paths to help others by sharing their burden. In turn, they must be willing to share ours.

It used to be said that the United States and England are only separated by a common language. The near-term future may see more separation of the two by new negotiations. There is the opportunity to improve relations with new negotiators who are not risk-averse.

Using past configurations as milestones can simplify future trade policy, but without mandatory orientation. Bilateral discussions between the United States and the United Kingdom must focus on building strength.

Global openness with reasonable partners, accompanied by transparency and the pursuit of common objectives and supported by balanced consumption are key paths for progress toward a better human condition.

CHAPTER 34

Global Medical Tourism

(With Nittaya Wongtada)

Medical tourism can be traced to 4000 BC when Greek pilgrims would sail abroad to seek the healing power of hot springs and baths. Over the past two decades, the industry encountered dramatic shifts.

Once wealthy patients from emerging economies sought treatments not available in their home countries. Since the new millennium, however, the flow of patients goes in the other direction. Rising health care costs prompt travelers from advanced economies to seek international destinations offering lower-cost or timelier alternatives to domestic care.

For instance, a spinal fusion in the United States costs an average of $110,000 in 2016. The same procedure could be done for $6,150 in Vietnam. Heart bypass surgery, which costs $123,000 in the United States in 2016, could be performed for $12,100 in Malaysia. For many patients from high-priced countries, the solution is clear—it pays to seek medical care abroad!

The size of such tourism has ballooned since the late 1990s. Its value ranges between $45.5 billion and $72 billion in 2017, with approximately 14–16 million patients seeking medical care beyond their countries' borders.

Modern medical tourism is a global phenomenon. Traditional models emphasized internationalization as an incremental procedure. But the industry surged after the Asian financial crisis of 1997, which drove hospitals in Malaysia, Singapore, and Thailand to seek patients from abroad. They had already undergone substantial modernization, catering to a domestic middle class that demanded medical services commensurate with their newly acquired wealth. With the economic downturn, however, a shrinking middle class could no longer afford these superior facilities. International clients provided a ready solution to an excess supply of private medical facilities.

The success of hospitals in Southeast Asia inspired other countries toward medical tourism. Regional hubs emerged due to advantages of geographical proximity and specialization. Malaysia and Singapore, for instance, received an influx of patients from Indonesia, while many patients in India came from Africa and the Middle East. Brazil, Costa Rica, and Mexico all benefitted from their proximity to the United States.

A clear pattern has emerged in the lifecycle of medical industries. First, countries in the developing world begin to offer services similar to those found in advanced economies. As new segments of international health care populations emerge, just like sun flowers, new medical tourism destinations grow toward the new opportunity. Close proximity to wealthy consumers constitute a competitive edge. To retain their market share, leading destinations formulate new strategies and options.

In order to survive growing competition, hospitals in emerging nations tend to implement two strategies. Since technologies stem from postindustrialized countries, most can only imitate. Their novelty comes from specialization in specific medical procedures. Doing few tasks very often improves capability, capacity, and efficiency, and thus improves reputational success.

However, this tactic may be ineffective as other hospitals develop similar capabilities. Consumer preferences will hinge on how closely services comply with their own cultural preferences and norms. Hospitals attract patients based on familiarity with local approaches and usages. Such an approach gives room for the increasingly recognized component of holistic healing.

It is important to understand how the lifecycle of hospitals continues to evolve. Different stakeholders—from governments to accreditation services to health care providers to patients themselves—will be affected by the expansion of the industry. For example, to date, there is still much unfounded reluctance to accept health care services offered by international sources. Once the industry manages to break out of restrictive domestic silos, a fundamental reconfiguration of service and cost will be the consequence. Let's look forward to that!

CHAPTER 35

Letting the Soul Lead the Way

To honor God in all we do, to help people develop, to pursue excellence, and to grow profitably are the espoused values of ServiceMaster Company, a leading company delivering world-class service. The first two items in its motto are the ends and the second two "to" are the means. Below are the thoughts of a practical nature, which help executives capture the opportunity to call on the soul for a strong foundation in our quickly changing times. Here are intermediary steps for marketers to re-approach the soul:

Understand the four new core areas of truthfulness, simplicity, expanded participation, and personal responsibility. These are every field's pillars for a shining business position. Frontline marketers need to understand how a product works and provide uncomplicated experiences to users. In the meantime, distance cannot mean abdication of responsibility. Having a positive boardroom culture where discussion and respect of different views is required. Though the chair of a multinational corporation may feel herself far removed from local issues, the locals themselves take all of the firm's actions very personally.

Introduce a mindful practice in the workplace. Leading corporations like Google, Intel, and General Mills have used the concept of mindfulness. Through meditation practice, speaker Paul Ryan in the House and Dean Almeida at Georgetown have also been working to reinvigorate core American values. Meditation is believed to not only unlock the productive habits of staff, but also to build conscious professionalism as well as leadership.

Consider the introduction of guiding key tenets in the educational curriculum of business schools. One approach could be the transference and implementation of Jesuit thought. Could one think of a reliable, productive, and high-quality mercenary as output of business schools? Education by members of the Society of Jesus could be characterized by the distinctive imperatives of ethic and honesty. When Ignatius of Loyola founded the religious order of the Jesuits almost 500 years ago, he expressly saw himself as establishing a service of special defenders and promoters of papal theological thought and clerical practice. He presented the vow of obedience and encouraged all members of the society to become "soldiers of God." At present, Jesuit colleges teaching business should offer no less than Ignatius intended. They need to ensure that those students they honor with an MBA degree are vigorous promoters and defenders of an honest and straightforward business mission and practice. For business, there is no need to call for ghost busters when engaging the service of a Jesuit MBA. Enhanced collaboration with Jesuit education could help future executives to know and see leadership, as well as clarify, even for distanced owners, the means and ends of international business.

A key auto industry executive, Bob Lutz, used to describe two kinds of people in automobile companies: carmakers and bean counters. Car guys are those who work at General Motors, Ford, or Chrysler during the day, and then work at night on their cars as a hobby. On weekends, they would race them. During their free time, they would talk cars with other car folks. That is what built General Motors and Detroit in general.

The rise of the nonmakers to positions of dominance in the domestic car industry almost destroyed the carmakers. While carmakers pursued manufacturing perfection for pleasure, nonmakers focused on financial manipulation over product excellence. As the Austrian-born English philosopher Wittgenstein stated, "A philosopher who is not taking part in discussions is like a boxer who never goes into the ring." It is time for all of us to approach the ring with slow steps, having prepared the body for the event, and letting the soul lead the way.

Sources

III. On Terrorism and Its Impact on International Business and Trade

Index

OTHER TITLES IN THE INTERNATIONAL BUSINESS COLLECTION

Tamer Cavusgil, Georgia State; Michael Czinkota, Georgetown; and Gary Knight, Willamette University, Editors

- *Creative Solutions to Global Business Negotiations, Second Edition* by Claude Cellich and Jain Subhash
- *Doing Business in Russia: A Concise Guide, Volume I* by Anatoly Zhuplev
- *Doing Business in Russia: A Concise Guide, Volume II* by Anatoly Zhuplev
- *Major Sociocultural Trends Shaping the Contemporary World* by K.H. Yeganeh
- *Globalization Alternatives: Strategies for the New International Economy* by Joseph Mark Munoz
- *Doing Business in the United States: A Guide for Small Business Entrepreneurs with a Global Mindset* by Anatoly Zhuplev, Matthew Stefl, and Andrew Rohm

Announcing the Business Expert Press Digital Library

Concise e-books business students need for classroom and research

This book can also be purchased in an e-book collection by your library as

- a one-time purchase,
- that is owned forever,
- allows for simultaneous readers,
- has no restrictions on printing, and
- can be downloaded as PDFs from within the library community.

Our digital library collections are a great solution to beat the rising cost of textbooks. E-books can be loaded into their course management systems or onto student's e-book readers. The **Business Expert Press** digital libraries are very affordable, with no obligation to buy in future years. For more information, please visit **www.businessexpertpress.com/librarians**. To set up a trial in the United States, please email **sales@businessexpertpress.com**.

.

www.ingramcontent.com/pod-product-compliance
Lightning Source LLC
Chambersburg PA
CBHW071839200326
41519CB00016B/4176